MEDEA

MEDEA'S FOLLY

Women, Relationships, and the Search for Intimacy

TANYA WILKINSON, PH.D.

PAGEMILL PRESS
A Division of Circulus Publishing Group, Inc.
Berkeley, California

MEDEA'S FOLLY:

Women, Relationships, and the Search for Intimacy

PUBLISHER: Tamara Traeder
EDITOR: Roy M. Carlisle
COPYEDITOR: Jean Blomquist
COVER DESIGN: Big Fish Design
INTERIOR DESIGN: Gordon Chun Design
TYPOGRAPHIC SPECIFICIATIONS: Body text is 11 point Adobe Caslon. Subheads are 7.5 point Frutiger Black. Myths and fairy tales are 12 point Bernhard Modern.

PRINTED IN THE UNITED STATES OF AMERICA

LIBRARY OF CONGRESS CATALOGING-IN-PUBLICATION DATA
Wilkinson, Tanya, 1952–
    Medea's folly : women, relationships, and the search for intimacy / Tanya Wilkinson
        p. cm.
    Includes bibliographical references (p. 190) and index.
    ISBN 1-879290-14-6 (pbk. : alk. paper)
    1. Women—Psychology.   2. Interpersonal relations.   3. Man-woman relationships.   4. Intimacy (Psychology).   I. Title.
HQ1206.W715   1998
158.2'082–dc21

98-9821
CIP

Distributed to the trade by Publishers Group West
10 9 8 7 6 5 4 3 2 1

DEDICATION

This book is for the women who have been and who are my students:

> It may not be true
> that one myth cancels another.
> Nevertheless, in a corner
> of the hem, where it will not be seen,
> where you will inherit
> it, I make this tiny
> stitch, my private magic.

Margaret Atwood, *Two-Headed Poems*

CONTENTS

Acknowledgments

Medea's Folly was inspired by conversations. Because of that, the book's beginnings parallel its themes: intimacy produces insight, interaction gives birth to knowledge. Therefore I must first thank all the people, friends, colleagues, students, clients, loved ones, and strangers, who take the time to talk to me.

A number of people gave me a more focused kind of help by reading and commenting on early drafts of *Medea*. Padma Catell, Phyllis Jackson, Marc Ellen Hamel, Carolyn Hall, Ann Parker, Marc Ellyn Garth, and Adrienne Amundsen cheerfully slogged through half-formed chapters and came up with clear, tactful feedback.

Without the support my friends and colleagues gave me when I published my first book, *Persephone Returns,* I would never have written a second. John Dyckman, John Klimek, Robert Hopcke, Paul Schwartz, Rusa Chiu, Gail Grynbaum, and Helen Wickes all went out of their way to give me recognition and encouragement. My colleagues (past and present) at the California Institute of Integral Studies were generous and heartening in their responses. My editor, Roy M. Carlisle, and my publisher, Tamara Traeder, have been unfailingly helpful with both books. I feel lucky to have found them (or to have been found by them). Finally, and always, my oldest friends, clump members and Thanksgiving diehards, provide the foundation, the ever-present acceptance, that makes risk-taking possible.

Myths, Fairy Tales, and Interviews

WOMEN AND THEIR SEARCH for intimacy is a vital and volatile topic, one that has inspired many books. Despite the reams of psychological theory, cultural analysis, and straightforward advice that have been written about the female quest for intimate relationships, that search continues to prompt questions and generate confusion. My own questions and my own confusion prompted the exploration that resulted in *Medea's Folly*.

I want to explain some aspects of my approach to this book. The main sources of information used in *Medea's Folly* are myths, fairy tales, interviews with three women (here called Cora, Lauren, and Bianca), and my own experiences. I asked my interviewees questions that were designed to corroborate or illustrate ideas I already had about the search for meaningful relationships in women's lives or ideas that came from my interpretation of the myths and fairy tales used in this work. If an interviewee told me something that contradicted an idea or insight I was pursuing, I generally abandoned the idea. The interviews do not meet the requirements of research as it is usually understood in my field. They do, however, meet the requirements of research that I once heard Catherine MacKinnon, the feminist lawyer, delineate at a public lecture. She said, "Feminist research is going out, finding some women, and asking them questions." The interviews are a form of collaborative inquiry, allowing me to explore the issues at hand with some checks and balances provided by the thoughtful women who agreed to be interviewed.

I did not use examples from my clinical work to elaborate my ideas because I do not want to pose women's quest for intimacy as a clinical problem. Women and their experiences are so easily pathologized in our culture, and especially in the field of psychology, that I wanted to take special pains to avoid even the appearance of diagnosing the quest for intimacy as a syndrome of some kind. I attempt to use a psychological viewpoint to illuminate the female search for meaningful relationships without making that search into a psychopathological problem. If I used examples from my psychotherapy practice, I would unavoidably leave the impression that the quest for intimacy is a psychotherapeutic issue.

It's true that women resort to psychotherapy a great deal more than men—approximately five times as much. I see this statistic as a by-product of the inevitable collision between a woman's sense of self and what Carol Gilligan calls "the wall of Western culture." Despite the obvious changes in our culture over the last twenty years, the persistent biases of our society still exert tremendous pressure on girls and women, seriously amplifying every developmental or circumstantial problem they have. As a consequence, women experience a lot of psychological suffering. It's true that women suffer a great deal in their quest for intimacy. Their suffering is emotional and psychological, and so psychotherapists are often called on to help them with their distress. However, as will become clear in the course of this book, I see their distress as more than personal in origin. Its sources are social, cultural, and collective, as well as individual.

In my experience, writing a book involves many struggles. For *Medea's Folly*, I struggled a great deal with the issue of generalization. I am uncomfortable with many works that I read because the author claims to speak for all women. Yet I do this myself, as you will find when you read on. For a time, I attempted to avoid generalized statements—the ones that start with "Women are . . ." or "Usually women feel . . ."—but I found that my writing path became impossibly convoluted, blocked with piles of modifiers, caveats, and disclaimers. So you will find many generalizations in these pages. To whom do they apply? Any woman for whom they fit. Please discard anything that doesn't fit. Immediately.

My generalizations are probably most suspect when it comes to women of color, gay women, and upper-class women. I am white (European-American?), straight, and I come from a working class background. I certainly believe that it is possible that some of my perceptions, concepts, and understandings will be useful to women whose life experiences I have not shared, but I do not wish to claim that they *will* be useful. I struggled with the possibility of including gay women in my interviews, and thus expanding the scope of my generalizations. However, in the end I felt that I would not be able to do such interviews justice. I simply do not know if my intuition about intimate partnerships, based in my own heterosexual experience, would hold.

Working with myths and fairy tales can also be a struggle.

C. G. Jung prompts us to approach these archetypal stories as sources of knowledge. He believed that myth and folklore, as products of the human imagination that had survived the tests of oral tradition as well as persisted through the centuries in print, contained insights about the psyche and particularly about the archetypal patterns that drive human development. These ancient insights have been largely lost to the contemporary Western psychologist. Diving into the myth of Medea and three fairy tales—"Bluebeard," "Fitcher's Bird," and "Elsa and the Evil Wizard"—I learned many new things, which I have tried to convey in the coming chapters. I also learned, or relearned since I have experienced learning this before, that these old stories provide constant surprises, prompting insights that take the author off on roads never anticipated in the original book outline. For this reason the process of writing this book was truly an exploration. It was only by delving into the meaning of the female quest for intimacy as fully as I could, by trying to understand as completely as I could what women are trying to do in that quest, that I could come, in the end, to any idea of what might be helpful. I have tried, in the text, to take the reader through that process of exploration so that the conclusions that sprang from it are as real to you as they were to me.

USING MYTHS AND FAIRY TALES

Why have I chosen myths and fairy tales to anchor my inquiry? What do these stories have to offer us? Stories, especially archetypal stories like myths and fairy tales, can provide unusual perspectives, giving access to knowledge that feels new but may be quite old. Narrative and image are gateways to the depths of the psyche, connecting habitual everyday consciousness to those aspects of human experience that are not very accessible to the intellect. The myth, as a form of imaginal "knowing," is more expansive and multilayered than linear, rational knowing. The portraits of women's lives in archetypal stories can lead us into open exploration, activating our search for meaning and self-knowledge. Such stories easily hold the contradictions and oppositions inherent in profound human experiences, helping us to avoid the temptation to polarize our understanding into simplistic, projection-laden analyses. Myths and fairy tales weave together the material, psychological, and spiritual worlds, giving us images which can contain these levels as they interact.

Finding a myth that resonates with a particular emotional and psychological situation and working with the episodes and images in the story can lead to unexpected insight. Because mythic narratives function metaphorically rather than rationally, they are particularly effective in accessing the wholeness which is potential in the archetypal self. According to Marie-Louise von Franz, myths and fairy tales tell us, in symbolic language and from a variety of angles, the story of the self.[a] Jung states that we may "define the Self as the totality of the conscious and unconscious psyche, but this totality transcends our vision. . . . It would be wildly arbitrary to restrict the self to the limits of the individual psyche, quite apart from the fact that we have not the least knowledge of those limits, seeing that they also lie in the unconscious. We should not be surprised if the empirical manifestations of unconscious contents bear all the marks of something illimitable, something not determined by time and space."[b] This means that the unconscious is a store-house of insight and knowledge that goes beyond the confines of any individual human being's experience.

In Jung's view, the self is both personal and transpersonal, a resource of transformative power that is accessed through the unconscious. These are resources that may be especially helpful in exploring the shadow aspect of the female quest for intimacy. This is an emotionally and politically sensitive topic that lends itself to preconceptions, bias, and reactivity. Using archetypal stories to explore such a thorny subject may help me to see around my own blind spots. Stories may help both author and reader to hold the inherent contradic-tions of this quest in mind, to see the light and the shadow without using one to cancel out the other.

As with all archetypal stories, the tales used in this book have great depth and lend themselves to many useful inter-pretations. The fact that I use a particular fairy tale or myth to reflect on my concerns about women and relationships does not mean that this is the only way to view those stories. Working with myths and fairy tales helps us to draw on resources within the unconscious. Those resources are uni-versal in the sense that anyone and everyone can gain inter-nal access to them. At the same time, the path to those resources of the unconscious are very particular to the indi-vidual. This is the paradoxical nature of the self. The stories I have chosen to work with give us images for the universal dimensions of internal resources. The reader's own personal story must be told, explored, and reflected on with the same respect as the archetypal tale. Only this will reveal the indi-vidual path which will be most helpful to each person.

I will be working with the myth of Medea and three fairy

tales, "Bluebeard," "Fitcher's Bird," and "Elsa and the Evil Wizard." "Fitcher's Bird" is recounted in full in chapter six and "Elsa and the Evil Wizard" is told in chapter seven. The stories of Medea and the fairy tale "Bluebeard" follow.

Medea

JASON was a prince whose inheritance had been usurped by his uncle Pelias. Pelias had murdered all other heirs to the throne except his brother, Aeson the rightful king, whom he kept in prison and Aeson's son, Jason. At his birth, in order to protect him, Jason's mother had proclaimed him stillborn and sent him away as an infant to Mount Pelion. When he was grown, Jason returned to his homeland and claimed his kingdom. King Pelias told him that before he could have his birthright, he must free his country from a curse by capturing the Golden Fleece.

Sailing on his ship, the *Argo*, Jason and his companions, the Argonauts, come to Colchis in search of the Golden Fleece. In order to win the prize, Jason must accomplish a number of fantastic and seemingly impossible tasks set by Aeetes, the King of Colchis. Jason must harness the fire-breathing, metal-hoofed bulls of Hephaestus, the blacksmith god, to a plow, plow a field with them, and sow the field with serpent's teeth. Fortunately for the Argonauts, the king's daughter, Medea, fell in love with Jason at first sight. Some of the gods who were interested in Jason's cause had persuaded Aphrodite's son, Eros (whom we now call Cupid), to shoot one of his arrows into her heart. Medea, as a sorceress and a priestess of Hecate, knew of a magic lotion which would protect Jason from the bulls. She gave it to him on the condition that she would sail with him on the *Argo* as his wife. Medea insisted that Jason swear a holy oath of fidelity to her.

Jason was successful in his labors, but the King of Colchis still did not wish to part with the Golden Fleece and confided his hesitancy to his daughter Medea. She secretly led Jason to the fleece hanging in the sacred grove behind the palace. Medea enchanted the fierce dragon her father had left to guard the fleece. The Argonauts stole the Golden Fleece and fled on the *Argo* with Medea, pursued by her father's fleet. Medea's half-brother, Apsyrtus, commanded the fleet. Jason and Medea lured him onto an island and murdered him, leaving their pursuers leaderless. Medea and Jason were then purified of the crime of murder by her Aunt Circe, the *Odyssey*'s famous island witch.

Medea carried with her the fabulous Cauldron of Regeneration. Dismembered animals and people were stewed in it and reborn with new power and vigor. After filling the teeming vessel with secret elements, "She mixed the whole concoction thoroughly, stirring it with a long withered branch . . . suddenly, as she moved the old stick round and round in the bowl of hot liquid, the branch grew green, clothed itself in leaves and, an instant later, was laden with heavy clusters of olives. Whenever the heat of the fire caused the froth to boil over out of the bronze cauldron, so that warm drops fell on the earth, the ground at that point grew green and flowers and soft grass sprang up." When they returned to Jason's homeland, Medea used her Cauldron of Regeneration to revitalize old Aeson, Jason's father, by dismembering him and submerging him in the boiling potion. "Quickly his hair and beard lost their whiteness, turning dark once more. The shriveled, neglected look of old age vanished. New flesh filled out his sagging wrinkles, and his limbs grew young and strong. The old man marveled at the change in himself, this was the Aeson of forty years ago." When Medea and Jason returned to Pelias's court with the Golden Fleece, Medea demonstrated her magic to Pelias and his daughters by cutting up an old sheep and cooking it in the cauldron. Out sprang a new lamb. She offered to renew the youth of Pelias, Jason's old uncle who had usurped Jason's throne, and Pelias's daughters dismembered him willingly. However, Medea refused to complete the spell and Pelias was not reborn. In this way, Jason avenged his uncle's betrayal of his father and himself.

Medea and Jason settled in Corinth, where Medea was the only surviving descendant of the Corinthian royal house. The Corinthians accepted them as king and queen. They ruled there for ten years, apparently happy, and had many children. Then Jason decided he wanted to marry a young and beautiful Theban princess, the daughter of the powerful tyrant Creon. His wife reminded him of his oath of loyalty, but he remained obstinate, claiming that a forced oath is invalid. Medea pointed out that he owed the

Corinthian throne to her, but Jason claimed that the Corinthians would support him because they liked him better than they liked her.

Medea, feigning acceptance, sent the princess a wedding gift, a robe which, when put on, burst into unquenchable flames. The princess ran in desperation through the wedding party, spreading the flames so that the palace, the wedding guests, and Creon were all consumed with the bride. Only Jason escaped the fire, by jumping from an upstairs window. Medea fled Corinth. Some say that to complete her revenge, she killed her children before she ran. Others say that she told her children to take refuge in Hera's temple, where the enraged Corinthians slaughtered them.

Medea flew from Corinth in a chariot drawn by winged dragons, steeds sprung from the Titans. First she flew to Thebes where she cured Heracles of the madness which had caused him to kill his children. Having killed the Theban princess whom Jason had wanted to marry, she could not stay in Thebes but flew on to Athens. The king there, Aegeus had sworn to shelter her if she was ever in need. He and Medea married. She lived in Athens until she was accused of attempting to poison Theseus, the heir to the throne. She traveled to Thessaly and Italy, where she is still worshipped as a goddess. She lived for a time in Asia Minor, where she was rumored to have married a king. Finally returning to Colchis with her son, whose father may have been Jason or may have been the Asian king, she helped her father regain his throne.

Jason, meanwhile, wandered homeless, cursed by

the gods for dishonoring their names when he broke his oath to Medea. In old age, he came once more to Corinth and sat down in the shadow of the prow of the *Argo*, remembering past glories and thinking of the disasters that had overwhelmed him. Suddenly, the wreck toppled forward and killed him. Medea never died but became immortal. She reigns in the Elysian fields, that part of the underworld where the virtuous are eternally content, unless they choose to be reborn.[c]

Bluebeard

THERE was a man who had fine houses, a great deal of silver and gold plate, and coaches plated all over with gold. But this man had a blue beard. He desired to marry one of his neighbor's beautiful daughters, but they did not want him because of his blue beard and because he had many wives already (although nobody knew what had become of them). Bluebeard, to engage their affection, took the family and their friends to his country house, showing them extravagant hospitality, denying them nothing. All of their time passed in feasting, mirth, and pleasure. In short order, the younger daughter began to think that his beard was not so blue and that he was a mighty civil gentleman. As soon as they returned home, the marriage was concluded.

After about a month of married life Bluebeard told his wife that he would be going on a journey to look after his affairs in the country.

"Here are the keys to my house," he said "the keys to all of the rooms, closets, and wardrobes are here. Go wherever you want, look into everything, except this one room, which I forbid you. If you go into it you will have my just anger and resentment."

She promised to obey. Soon after Bluebeard left for his journey, his wife invited her friends and relatives to view her opulent new home. They explored and admired every richly appointed chamber. After they left, however, Bluebeard's wife was overcome with curiosity. She could not rest until she opened the door to the forbidden room.

At first she could see little, for the windows were shuttered. Then she began to perceive that the floor was all clotted over with blood, on which lay the bodies of several dead women, ranged against the walls. These were Bluebeard's past wives. She was overcome with fear, and the key, which she had pulled out of the lock, fell from her hand onto the bloody floor. She picked it up, relocked the door, and fled upstairs to try and recover herself. She noticed then that the key was stained with blood and no matter what she cleaned it with, the stain would not come off.

When Bluebeard returned his wife did everything she could to convince him that she was glad to see him. Soon, however, he asked for the house keys and noticed that the key to the forbidden room was missing. After making many excuses and delays, his wife was forced to hand over the key. Bluebeard examined it very closely.

"How comes this blood upon the key?" he asked her.

"I do not know!" cried the poor woman.

"I very well know," replied Bluebeard. "You went into the forbidden room, and now you must die, madam, and that presently."

"If I must die," she said, "give me some time to say my prayers."

"I give you a quarter of an hour."

She spent that quarter hour anxiously looking out for the arrival of her brothers, who had intended to come that day. At last, just as she saw their dust on the road, her husband came in. Taking hold of her hair, he lifted his sword, intending to take her head while she implored him for her life. At this very instant, a loud knocking at the gate caused Bluebeard to stop. His wife's brothers, one a musketeer and the other a dragoon, rushed in with drawn swords. Chasing Bluebeard down, they ran him through and left him dead.[d]

CHAPTER ONE

Women and the Search for Intimacy

M Y OFFICE is a classic San Francisco room with high ceilings and Edwardian paneling. Large windows fill the office with light. Women come to this room, sit on the overstuffed sofa, and tell me about their lives. For the most part, this means that they tell me about their relationships, often talking more about others than about themselves. My supervisors in graduate school taught me to call this kind of behavior "resistance." They saw such talk as an avoidance, a way of evading the "real" work of therapy, that is, the work of examining the self. For a long time I saw it that way too. Now I'm not so sure. Now I think that women talk about relationships in order to talk about themselves—that is, to more fully understand themselves and their lives.

As I listen to women talking about their spouses, children, friends, co-workers, all of the people that they see as their partners in life, I realize that something complicated is going on. In response to their stories, I feel both admiration and impatience. What an amazing capacity for love they have! What poor judgment they have! Or is it poor judgment? Why are they willing to put up with so much garbage? Women are searching for something important in relationships. They seem to be on a *quest* and, like the knights who sought the Holy Grail, they are willing to put up with a lot to continue that quest. Sometimes that willingness, that perseverance, looks like poor judgment. Sometimes it *is* poor judgment. Yet women have a talent for relationship. Why, then, do they sometimes use this talent wisely and at other times unwisely?

FEMALE DEVOTION TO RELATIONSHIPS

Our everyday experiences confirm that women are especially dedicated to their relationships. We look around and find that women are in the majority at PTA meetings, and at meetings of other organizations focused on family and children. We read the advice columns and find that the vast majority of letters requesting advice on preserving or improving relationships come from women. It's axiomatic in the publishing industry that relationship books aimed at men are all bought by women for male partners. Typically we see women working hard at establishing, maintaining, and improving intimacy.

Women have a talent for building and maintaining relationships. A woman's strong belief in the importance of relationships is manifested and enacted in her use of language, in her moral choices, and in most of her personal decisions. Harvard psychologist Carol Gilligan, in her groundbreaking study of women's moral development, concludes from her research that "women perceive and construe social reality differently than men," "these differences center around experiences of attachment and separation," and "women's sense of integrity seems to be entwined with an ethic of care, so that to see themselves as women is to see themselves in a relationship of connection."[1] Consider the implications of the assertion that for women "to see themselves as women is to see themselves in a relationship of connection." Is connection intrinsic to identity for women? If so, what might this mean in terms of behavior?

Consider the story of Diana, Princess of Wales. From her entrance into the glare of public life at nineteen until her tragic death at thirty-six, her life was entirely and completely defined by her connections to her husband, her lovers, her in-laws, her sons. Her worth as a person, in the eyes of the public and in the estimation of the media, rose and fell according to how caring she seemed to be. Her exalted posthumous status springs from how warm and intimate she seemed to be with the most vulnerable people of the world —the sick, the poor, the war-torn, children, the elderly. Diana's position as the perennial victim of a powerful, cold husband and an overwhelming host of in-laws was elevated, after death, to saintly martyrdom. I believe that her fate evoked an amazing outpouring of feeling because she played out, on a mythic, grand scale, the almost universal quest that women in the Western world pursue—the quest for meaning in life through intimacy.

Did Diana's death overtake her just as she was about to fulfill this quest in her relationship with Dodi Fayed? This seems to be widely believed, even though her relationship with him had been widely ridiculed before her death. It will never be possible to discern the truth of the assumption that she had finally found true intimacy, but the readiness with which people embraced the idea is important. As women search throughout life for the seemingly elusive prize of the right relationship, they continually feel that it has been snatched out of their hands by fate, by another woman, by their own mistakes or imperfections. They often feel this even about relationships which last a lifetime. Diana's royal marriage, so frequently called a fairy tale, elevated her experience of the female search for perfect intimacy to the level of myth. Our detailed knowledge of her personal life and the intense drama of her death made her story legendary. The extravagance of public mourning provided a ritualized way for people to participate in Diana's mythic drama. But why was it so meaningful to be able to participate in her story—to stand for hours to catch a glimpse of the coffin, or to stay up late into the night, watching a funeral taking place on another continent?

If Diana was "the Queen of Hearts," if her life was a "candle in the wind," why was that so profoundly touching? I think that her very public disappointments in her search for intimacy, her rejection and humiliation at the hands of the other royals, her enormous mistakes with lovers, her sparkling social successes, her obvious devotion to her children all gave weight and importance to the story of women in our culture. Diana could have come to my office to tell me her story and, minus the titles, it would have resonated with the stories of most of my female clients. They so desperately wish to be the queen of someone's heart, and the impermanence of that position is so like a candle in the wind. Diana's passion play lifted these everyday female realities, usually made to seem as trivial as the subject of a "soap opera," into a realm of global significance. Her quest for meaningful intimacy, the ups and downs of her relationships, her ability to care and connect were worth photographing, documenting, debating, and eulogizing. By implication, this elevated the common woman's quest for intimacy. Her own ups and downs, successes and failures in relationships were given significance, even though the common woman's drama is played out on a small stage, in mundane interactions and everyday conversations.

DEVOTION TO CLOSENESS

By examining those everyday conversations, Deborah Tannen's linguistic research tells us something about the way in which this mythic quest for meaningful relationships guides women's behavior. She finds that women consciously and unconsciously pursue conversational strategies that reflect a desire for closeness above all else. For instance, the women Tannen studied, when presented with conflict in a conversation, would attempt to find common ground for everyone involved in the conversation, even at the expense of their own point of view. The majority of women she observed tried, directly and indirectly, to find a way to unite the conflicting opinions, while the majority of men tried to make sure that their own opinion prevailed. From many similar observations, Tannen concludes that a typical woman approaches the world as "an individual in a network of connections [in which] conversations are negotiations for closeness . . . [T]hey [women] try to protect themselves from others' attempts to push them away. . . . Life is . . . a struggle to preserve intimacy and avoid isolation."[2] Tannen and Gilligan are part of a larger trend in contemporary gender difference research, a trend that tends to confirm the existence of certain psychological differences between men and women, differences which have, in the recent past, been considered pernicious stereotypes. This research finds that women are generally more active than men in facilitating relationships and experience intimacy as more primary to life than men do.

Historically feminism has critiqued this role for women. In Betty Friedan's classic book, *The Feminine Mystique,* she warned women against the pitfalls of defining their identities through their relationships. In an analysis of fiction appearing in women's magazines of the fifties and sixties she found that the typical happy ending featured "the disappearance of the heroine as a separate self." It appeared that, for the ideal woman in popular fiction, "the end of the road is togetherness."[3] Friedan showed that women were given explicit instruction in articles or advice columns and implicit instruction through images and narratives about having successful relationships. The essence of these teachings was that togetherness requires selflessness for *women,* though apparently not for men. For women, attention to the self appeared to be opposed to the fulfillment of intimacy. This dichotomy was taken as a given both by the culture at large and by feminist critics of that culture, with the dominant culture upholding togetherness as the best female option and feminists upholding self as the new priority. The opposition of self and relationship became a central theme in early feminist theory and in feminist fiction such as Marilyn French's best-selling novel of 1977, *The Women's Room.*[4]

Feminist psychologists soon began trying to move past the dichotomy of self vs. relationship. Nancy Chodorow's influential 1978 book, *The Reproduction of Mothering,* was a discourse on the consequences of gender differences in child rearing.[5] Chodorow claimed that, because girls experienced an uninterrupted identification with and attachment to their mothers, they have a more developed sense of empathy than boys, who must cut off their closeness with their mothers in order to develop a socially acceptable gender identity. Using psychoanalytic concepts, Chodorow attempted to show that, while this increased empathy made girls and women appear less autonomous in relationships, it should also make their sense of self, firmly based in identification with the mother, more secure. Comparable stances were taken by a number of feminist psychologists. Eventually a school of psychological thought called the Relational School emerged that explored this and other similar ideas about the psychology of women.

Jean Baker Miller, a pioneering theorist in the Relational School of psychology, asserts that "the girl's sense of self-esteem is based in feeling that she is a part of relationships and is taking care of those relationships. This is very different from the components of self esteem as usually described. . . . [T]he girl and woman often feel a sense of effectiveness as arising out of emotional connectedness. . . . This is very different from a sense of effectiveness [or power] based in lone action and in acting against or over others."[6] Miller is positing a form of self-development which is entwined with relationship rather than opposed to it. When she compares woman's emotional connectedness to power based in "acting against or over others," she seems to be referring to a type of power which is culturally associated with men. She seems to hint at the moral superiority of the female approach. This theme, the moral superiority of women, has gained considerable ground in recent years.

The female talent for relationship seems to have moved, in twenty-five years or so of feminist analysis, from being a problem for women (according to Friedan) to being an advantage for women (in current literature). This kind of turnabout, in regard to the female affinity for togetherness, is not limited to feminists. Western civilization has, in general, alternately beatified and demonized the woman who is dedicated to relationships. For example, the selfless mother who focuses intensely and exclusively on her relationships with her family may be depicted as a savior to her children, as in a sentimental movie like *I Remember Mama.* On the other hand such a mother might also show up as a devouring monster, as in Philip Roth's book, *Portnoy's Complaint.* These paired opposites occur in portrayals of the devoted wife, sister, daughter, girlfriend; women who from one angle are sanctified redeemers, from another side appear in diabolical form, as relational vampires.

Currently several influential branches of feminist thought are leaning strongly toward the idealized side of this polarity. Implications of or direct statements attesting to the moral superiority of women are present in work from the Relational School of psychology, from proponents of goddess spirituality, in the writings of ecofeminists and others. This commentary tends to portray female empathy as a wonderful gift that could save humankind, if not the planet itself. Typical statements attribute special insight to women, as in Charlene Spretnak's comment that "it is our refusal to banish feelings of interrelatedness and caring" [that will enable women to] find our way out of the technocratic alienation and nihilism surrounding us by cultivating and honoring our direct connections with nature."[7] This comment, just one of many, attributes a special kind of wisdom to women, a kind of feminist feminine mystique.

Women in these writings are envisioned as resources of togetherness: "We are . . . aware children of mother earth . . .

loving kin to all our relatives in this biosphere."[8] Women may be portrayed as central to a coming new age: "Women are creating a new society. We are using intellect, intuition, politics, magic, and art to restructure existing institutions and invent new ones . . . . Women are intimately involved with life."[9] Or, more blatantly, "The future is female."[10] Many simpler versions of these ideas show up in popular culture, where they are usually conveyed in stories about the redemptive power of the gift of a woman's unconditional love. Of course these ideas skirt perilously close to old stereotypes. As one unconvinced commentator put it, "The nineteenth-century Angel in the House has become the Savior of the World,"[11] referring to the old Victorian notion that women hold an angelic sensibility that is unavailable to men and that will sanctify those they love.

THE SHADOW OF THE TALENT FOR RELATIONSHIP

Is this simply the latest swing between the poles of the Western world's view of women and relationships? Perhaps, but it also reflects a denied reality. Women's orientation toward relationship has a light aspect and a shadow aspect. Both aspects are real, but typically only one side is attended to at a time. To have a large capacity for empathy and a facility for togetherness is, indeed, a gift. However, as most women have experienced at some time, the bright light of this gift casts a deep shadow. I believe it is the unacknowl-edged double nature of women's focus on intimacy, the fact that its power is both generative and destructive, that causes it to be alternately idealized and feared.

To the extent that the shadow cast by woman's gift for fostering relationships has been acknowledged, it has been portrayed as it appears to and affects others, chiefly men, thus the prevalence of the image of the devouring relational woman, the "man trap." But the way the shadow affects women themselves, the holders of the gift, is quite different from the way it affects the receiver of the gift. The shadow effects of a woman's strong focus on relationships, for the woman herself, has been generally ignored. Diana, Princess of Wales, is revered, especially since her death, for her gift of emotional connection, her willingness and ability to establish closeness—with AIDS patients, land-mine victims, her sons, the public at large. But was it her intense dependence on this very ability, her gift of emotional connection, that left her open to victimization in her relationships with her husband, her royal in-laws, her exploitive, publicity-seeking friends, and the public itself?

Diana shared this reality—that a dedication to relationships is both light and dark in its impact—with women in general. That women habitually use their relationship skills and their dedication to intimacy to maintain relationships that have little or no basis in true compatibility is the shadow side of the female gift for facilitating relationships. The shadow of intimacy, in a typical heterosexual relationship, results from the mating of a masculine shadow with this feminine shadow. The masculine shadow is the tendency to use intimacy as a convenience, and the intimate partner as an object of use. The coming together of these two shadows can make a close relationship into a destructive, victimizing force.

CHAPTER TWO

Looking for Love in All the Wrong Places

THE SHADOW aspect of the female affinity for relationship as experienced by women themselves—the use of relationship skills and dedication to intimacy to maintain relationships that have little or no basis in real compatibility—can be illuminated by looking at the connection between it and its counterpart, the masculine shadow. The masculine shadow is powerfully embodied in the man who preys on women. A very old French fairy tale features a character who is familiar to us from our daily news: the predatory male and domestic tyrant. His name in the tale is Bluebeard and his story begins like this:

THERE was a man who had fine houses, a great deal of silver and gold plate, and coaches plated all over with gold. But this man had a blue beard. He desired to marry one of his neighbor's beautiful daughters, but they did not want him because of his blue beard and because he had many wives already (although nobody knew what had become of them). Bluebeard, to engage their affection, took the family and their friends to his country house, showing them extravagant hospitality, denying them nothing. All of their time passed in feasting, mirth, and pleasure. In short order, the younger daughter began to think that his beard was not so blue and that he was a mighty civil gentleman. As soon as they returned home, the marriage was concluded.[1]

Interestingly, this ancient tale gives a fairly accurate description of one of the ways that abusive husbands today lure their spouses into oppressive, dangerous relationships—marriages in which, as psychiatrist Judith Herman puts it, the "victim is taken prisoner gradually through courtship."[2] Whether the medium of courtship is material (lavishing the targeted woman with gifts) or emotional (lavishing her with attention and praise), it is striking that Bluebeard's method of overcoming womanly resistance is indistinguishable from a type of romantic courtship we often see in the movies, such as Robert Redford's approach in the movie *Indecent Proposal.*

A German variation of the Bluebeard story called "Fitcher's Bird" begins in a slightly different way: *There was once a wizard who took the form of a poor man, and went to houses and begged and caught pretty girls.*[3] This is an alternate strategy of seduction in which engendering compassion and pity is the primary draw. This strategy is also common at the beginning of abusive domestic relationships. Whether consciously or unconsciously, the predatory suitor presents himself as a focus for help and redemption, possibly pursuing a combined strategy of showering the object of desire with attention and presents while simultaneously showing an urgent neediness that evokes sympathy. Women often believe that they are living out the story of "Beauty and the

Beast," i.e., that love and acceptance will bring about a transformation of beastliness into princeliness, but they wake up to find that they are one of Bluebeard's wives. And what happens to his wives? Returning to the old story we find that the younger daughter has married the generous gentleman and, left alone in his palatial home, she goes into a room he has forbidden her to enter. There she sees that the floor is all clotted over with blood, on which lay the bodies of several dead women. These are Bluebeard's past wives.[4]

As we know from reading the newspaper and watching the movie of the week on TV, this bloody fate may be literal for the wife of a contemporary Bluebeard. The regularity with which women are killed by their partners is impressive—4,000 women in America every year, according to Blue Shield.[5] But the story of Bluebeard does not just tell us something about assaultive and murderous husbands. Bluebeard's courtship technique, his assumption that he sets the terms in his relationship, and his easy willingness to discard any spouse who does not accommodate to those terms, are all recognizable factors in everyday, nonviolent heterosexual relationships. These are recognizable factors, for instance, in the marriage of Prince Charles and Diana, Princess of Wales. Dazzled by her prospective husband's glorious outer trappings, Diana entered into a marriage run entirely on her husband's terms. When she began to resist those terms, she was summarily stripped of marriage and title. Prince Charles, although clearly not a violent person, took a Bluebeard's stance toward his wife's individuality, needs, and growth. She was valuable, apparently, only when she followed the palace rules. No regard was given to how she felt about those rules, or if those rules were good for her.

In the absence of actual physical injury to the woman, the image of Bluebeard's dismembered wives may symbolize a psychological fate, representing the dismembered hopes and dreams, wasted potential, constricted development, and self-hatred that result from oppressive relationships. The injuries to Diana's self-esteem, her eating disorders, her anger and distress were all well documented and are not untypical in such relationships. Whether the injuries suffered by the partner of a Bluebeard are physical, psychological, or both, we are faced with a pressing question: What would make a woman who is not a character in a fairy tale fall for a Bluebeard's strategies?

The typical answer to this question focuses on the weaknesses and vulnerabilities that might leave a woman open to abusive manipulation. Put in general terms, the usual explanation emphasizes an exploited woman's negative traits or bad circumstances, traits springing either from personal history or social inequity. A political activist may attribute a woman's vulnerability to lack of appropriate laws and law enforcement. A sociologist might see economic dependence on the problematic partner as the primary factor. Most psychologists would think that low self-esteem, resulting from an abusive upbringing, is the most likely source of a susceptibility to destructive relationships. The bottom line in all of these theories (and others like them), however sympathetically it might be put, is that there is a serious flaw in the woman's circumstances, or in the woman herself, and this flaw has produced her attachment to the exploitive relationship.

It is neat and tidy to believe that only negative traits

motivate certain women to fall for the predatory and abusive male, the Bluebeard. Seen from this point of view, whatever notion the woman may have of redeeming her partner through love is mere rationalization, a conscious gloss on an unconscious masochism. At best, interpretations of such a woman's behavior that are based on legal, economic, or psychological deficiencies are partial explanations, accounting for some percentage of cases. But these hypotheses do not fully account for the well-noted persistence of exploitive relationships. In fact, women who have been adequately protected by the law, who have economic resources, and who exhibit strong self-esteem in other areas of life frequently return to destructive relationships, often believing that, with one more try, Beauty will transform the Beast. This behavior baffles us. Why would women act this way?

THE STRUGGLE TO PRESERVE INTIMACY

Exploited and abused women often act against their own interests and those of their children, but they do this not simply because of personal frailty or social disempowerment. There are also strengths, or relational capacities, which are more common to women than to men, that prompt women to ignore danger, rationalize bad behavior in loved ones, and hope for change in hopeless situations. It is my view that women's talent for relationship predisposes them to avoid a clear-eyed assessment of loved ones, sometimes for a tragically long time. Their dedication to the quest for intimacy interferes with normal self-protection. This is one of the shadow aspects of the priority women give to togetherness. It is the dangerous, unacknowledged side of their gift for fostering relationships.

Earlier I quoted psychologist Carol Gilligan, who said that "women perceive and construe social reality differently than men," "these differences center around experiences of attachment and separation," and "women's sense of integrity seems to be entwined with an ethic of care."[6] If Gilligan's research is valid, then women who stay in a certain kind of exploitive relationship may be trying to preserve their integrity, and not simply acting out a scenario of self-hatred or self-destruction. Furthermore, if we take Tannen's research conclusions seriously, namely that women "try to protect themselves from others' attempts to push them away" and that for them "life is . . . a struggle to preserve intimacy and avoid isolation,"[7] then women who persist in problematic relationships are struggling for their own priorities and protecting themselves from the danger they perceive as paramount—the disruption of intimacy. Women seem to find it difficult to know the difference between a Beast, who can be changed by the devotion of a Beauty, and a Bluebeard, who will use love and loyalty as a venue for manipulation and exploitation. In some cases, this confusion can be traced to serious inadequacies in a woman's social circumstances, support systems, self-regard, or even character. But not in all cases. What can these other cases teach us about women and intimacy?

THE DUPLICITOUS PROFESSOR AND THE SEDUCED STUDENT

Stories of women who choose a relationship over the dictates of "good sense," regardless of principles or consequences, are common. Extreme examples of women who foster and maintain relationships with batterers and murderers, with literal Bluebeards, show up regularly in the daily news. More mundane examples of women who allow themselves to be betrayed or belittled by spouses, lovers, children, bosses, and friends and who not only endure this treatment, this emotional dismemberment, but reward it with love and vigorous service, can be found in nearly everyone's circle of acquaintance. The *New York Review of Books* described one such relationship like this: "A duplicitous professor falls for an exotic student and uses his position to seduce her: the naive student is bamboozled and falls deeply in love. Twenty years later the duplicitous professor needs the help of the seduced student to restore his public reputation and his finances. . . . [T]he student lacks the good sense and self-respect to tell him to get lost, and devotes herself to managing the restoration of his finances and reputation until both die twenty-five years later."[8]

The seduced student in question was Hannah Arendt, a German Jew who fled Nazi Germany in 1933. She went on to write powerful, controversial commentary on the origins of totalitarianism in her book of the same title and on the nature of evil as it manifested in the Nazi regime in *Eichman in Jerusalem*.[9] The duplicitous (and married) professor was Martin Heidegger, who, some think, was the most influential philosopher of the twentieth century. A few years after the affair with Arendt, Heidegger embraced the Nazi party. He never publicly explained or apologized in any effective way for his complicity with that genocidal regime. Despite Heidegger's personal betrayal of Arendt in their love affair and his larger betrayal of both her people and his own integrity, Arendt did indeed do her best to rehabilitate him in the eyes of the world after the Nazis were defeated.

In 1995, Elzbieta Ettinger's book *Hannah Arendt/Martin*

Heidegger was published.[10] In the last months of that year and early months of 1996, several reviews of the book and articles concerning Arendt and Heidegger appeared. The commentary in the reviews and articles shared a certain judgmental tone, exemplified here by Alan Ryan in the *New York Review of Books:* "[Arendt] was a public moralist, never shy about the lies and self-deceptions of politicians, journalists, and other intellectuals. If she did not see through [Heidegger], that is disturbing. If she saw through him and conspired to protect him from his critics, that is more disturbing." And, on a harsher note, Ryan writes, "Ought she not to have remained unreconciled with him after the war and done her best to see that he was frozen out of the scholarly community?"[11]

This attitude is echoed by Robert Wistrich in his review in *Commentary:* "Arendt's eagerness to renew the friendship with Heidegger seems little short of baffling. . . . [She] rhapsodizes over her rapprochement with Heidegger." The reviewer is particularly horrified by the fact that Arendt referred to her reunion with Heidegger as "a confirmation of a whole life" and accuses her of "what was in effect a deliberate effort to whitewash his Nazi past." He concludes, "The story's most troubling aspect is the extent of Arendt's submissiveness to Heidegger."[12]

This submissiveness was a recurrent but not altogether consistent theme in the relationship. Arendt was eighteen when she went to the University of Freiburg and met Martin Heidegger. He was an idolized figure on campus, a thirty-five-year-old charismatic professor who soon began to shower her with flattering, erudite, seductive letters. She was vulnerable to seduction because of her youth, because of her position as a student (in that time and place a much more deferential position than it is now), because of her desire to assimilate fully into German culture (a desire that seemed to be shared by many German Jews at the time) and in the fact that she was female in an almost exclusively male intellectual world. To be marked as special by Heidegger, to be courted by him, was enticing. He made the rules, she followed them. Most of the time.

Heidegger made much of the "spiritual" connection between himself and Arendt. He said he wanted her as muse and confidante, for he felt alone in his quest for truth. She alone could be trusted. Here we see a woman being drawn into a dangerous situation through a display of riches, in this case the riches of the mind, of culture, of spirit—the sort of wealth most valuable to Hannah Arendt. Bluebeard's method of conquest is, in this instance, translated from the material to the cerebral. In addition, a sophisticated turn on the poor beggar disguise of the "Fitcher's Bird" variation of Bluebeard is being played out. The great man was in need, deprived of feminine inspiration and support. Arendt could serve as no other could, if only she saw and understood his need. In fact, Heidegger had young mistresses and female devotees both before and after his affair with Arendt, as well as a wife who was well positioned in the Nazi Party and very helpful with his career. This, too, is reflective of the fairy tale: the manipulator has done it all before and will do it again. Even if his need for female sacrifice is psychologically real, it is also apparently insatiable. No one seems to notice the girls who are used or used up. No one intervenes.

For a time, Hannah Arendt was able to explore the intellectual and cultural riches presided over by Martin Heidegger. She followed his stringent rules about writing letters, meetings, and conversation. When Arendt made efforts to build an emotional life away from Heidegger by transferring to another university and seeing a man her own age who wanted to marry her, he met this challenge to his ability to control the terms of the relationship by asserting his superior understanding. He convinced her that their continued affair, if seen in the correct spiritual light, need not adversely affect her ability to form a romantic relationship that could have a future. The fact that she accepted this view illuminates both her naive youth and Heidegger's powers of persuasion. Arendt explored Heidegger's realm, the mansion of German culture and learning, carefully following his rules, just as Bluebeard's wife roamed his castle, exploring the riches that drew her into the relationship. But, of course, these cultural riches were not really Arendt's. She was there on sufferance, subject to stringent constraints, in a mansion that was both opulent and full of death.

Was there a point when Arendt disobeyed? Did she enter the forbidden room and, like Bluebeard's wife, witness the bloody chamber, the murder hidden in the treasure? There were several points in the relationship which could have provided this kind of revelation. In 1928, when Heidegger was appointed to a prestigious chair at the university, he broke off his affair with Arendt. He was achieving recognition beyond academia with the publication of *Being and Time* and perhaps had more reason to fear exposure. Also there was another muse, another devoted intelligent young woman, waiting in the wings. Arendt was devastated by the abrupt, unilateral nature of the dissolution of their intimacy, but within the year she again was writing to Heidegger and calling his love "the blessing of my life." Apparently his personal betrayal was not shocking enough to shake her idealization of her exploitive mentor. But Heidegger was yet to go on to larger forms of betrayal.

In 1929, Heidegger wrote a letter to the German Ministry of Education warning of the "Judaization" of the university and the danger it presented to German spiritual life. This letter was his first direct statement, on record, of anti-Semitic and pro-Nazi sentiment and, of course, it suggests the exclusion of Jewish scholars like Hannah Arendt from university life. Although Arendt could not have read the letter, comparable rumors about her old lover's political views apparently reached her at her new university, for she wrote to Heidegger to challenge him about his stance toward Jews. He replied with a string of rationalizations, claiming that others had "slandered" him. He portrayed himself as a victim and implied that Arendt had betrayed him by believing such libel. Since he had already written the "Judaization" letter to the Ministry of Education, he was being duplicitous, at the very least. (Interestingly, the defensive letter to Arendt resembles in tone, form, and structure letters Heidegger sent to her rationalizing his personal behavior during their affair and is also similar to the material he presented to the Denazification Board after the war.) Arendt was once more convinced of Heidegger's integrity and resumed an admiring correspondence with him until 1933. She agreed once again to accept his direction, to avoid looking in the forbidden room.

In 1933, Heidegger assumed the rectorship of the University of Freiburg. He gave a now notorious, but then quite popular, inaugural speech in which he supported the Nazi agenda and wore the swastika. One of his official acts of that year was to send a letter to his former teacher Edmund Husserl, the revered founder of phenomenology, forbidding him to enter the grounds of the university because he was a Jew. Husserl had previously held Heidegger's own professorial chair and, as Heidegger's mentor, had been instrumental in securing it for his protégé. Husserl reportedly was devastated by Heidegger's behavior. Hannah Arendt left Germany in 1933, lived in other parts of Europe, and eventually emigrated to the United States. She severed all relationship with Martin Heidegger. She later wrote to a mutual friend "[B]ecause I know that this letter and this signature all but killed him [Husserl], I cannot but regard Heidegger as a potential murderer."

It seemed that Arendt had finally disobeyed the rules and allowed herself to see the bloody chamber, to grasp the damage Heidegger had done. She stayed clear about what she had seen for at least sixteen years, putting Heidegger's betrayal of Husserl in print in 1946 in an article entitled "What is Existence Philosophy?" and, in a personal letter, calling Heidegger's early post-war excuses "nothing but foolish lies with, it seems to me, a pronounced pathological streak. But that's an old story." (Here she seems to refer to her personal experience with him.) This stance lasted until she agreed, in response to a persuasive letter from him, to meet with Heidegger in Germany in 1950. Although Heidegger never recanted his Nazi past, after that meeting, Arendt recanted her opinion of his past.

On her return to New York, she wrote letters to influential people, saying that her published statements about Heidegger's Nazi past were all based on "rumor" and should be considered inaccurate. Arendt became Heidegger's unpaid agent and editor in America. She spent time with Heidegger's wife, an unrepentant Nazi functionary. She helped to arrange the sale of Heidegger's manuscripts and tried to effect reconciliation with mutual friends who would not forgive Heidegger for his behavior. Indeed, as Elzbieta Ettinger states, "Once the relationship was reestablished between the master and his disciple, there was nothing Arendt would not do for him." When questioned by her husband or others, she made excuses for Heidegger, trying to shift blame for his actions to his wife, or she railed against a supposed conspiracy of younger German philosophers for continued "rumors" of Heidegger's oppressive acts during his rectorship. (These were not rumor but documented fact.) She had once again accepted his image of himself as the lonely, misunderstood genius and the image of herself as his indispensable muse. It is as if Bluebeard's wife went into the forbidden room, saw the carnage, closed the door, and decided it wasn't real.

Think of the women you know who have done just what Hannah Arendt did. Perhaps their partners' betrayals did not have the historical proportion of Heidegger's betrayal, but the form of the story probably seems familiar to you. If you are a woman, perhaps you have done this yourself or are doing it now. To put the story in raw or simple form: a woman who does not seem to be a fool forms a relationship with a person who shows prima facie evidence of questionable character and who, sooner or later, betrays her. She does not take enduring steps to protect or distance herself from this hurtful person but instead seeks to preserve the relationship and give service to the betrayer. Whether this woman is yourself or someone you know, you may very well find yourself suffering from the same impatience expressed in the reviews of the book about Arendt and Heidegger. Inwardly, and sometimes outwardly, you find yourself saying, "Why is this woman acting like a fool?"

At the time these various reviews and essays about Arendt and Heidegger were published, I had some conversations with people who had read them. These conversations had a slightly less righteous but still bewildered tone. In essence people asked, "How could someone as sharp, smart, and articulate as Hannah Arendt act like this?" Because I am both a psychotherapist and a feminist, they sometimes expected me to answer this question. I found myself blurting out, "Why do we expect Hannah Arendt to behave differently from most other women, whether she was smart or not?" The failure to draw a clear line with hurtful, even dangerous partners, does not necessarily result from immaturity, from lack of intelligence or "good sense," or even from low self-esteem. As one commentator said, "It just won't do to reduce Hannah Arendt's failure to judge Heidegger as harshly as he deserved to an inability to get over a girlish crush."[13] Indeed, it won't do. In my clinical experience, the tendency to ignore and rationalize bad behavior in loved ones is a trait which is more prevalent in women than in men, and it is a trait that crosses levels of intelligence and self-esteem. In fact, I see it as a normal part of the feminine gender role. It is the shadow side of the female gift for facilitating relationships, the persistent downside of the quest for intimacy.

If we define normal as common or typical, Hannah Arendt was behaving normally for a woman when she dealt with Heidegger as she did. When an obviously brilliant, thoughtful, and accomplished woman behaves like a "regular" woman in a questionable relationship, we are shocked. Something about women and relationships, something about the hazards of the female quest for intimacy, something that we have rationalized or simply ignored, becomes apparent. Something in the shadow is brought into the light.

What makes a woman imagine that a Bluebeard is a possible partner? What special thing do women think is going to happen in an intimate partnership with such a man that will change him? Do they see themselves as having a special power, a power that will make the impossible partner possible? I don't think so. I think that something more complex is going on. When a woman has made a strong attachment to a man, she begins to experience his behavior as meaningful about herself rather than meaningful about him. This is one of the most damaging affects of the shadow side of the female devotion to relationships.

The fairy tale "Bluebeard" and its variations as well as the myth of Medea, which we will look at in the next chapter, can help us to explore the shadow side of women and relationships.

My use of the story of Medea might at first seem puzzling, in that she is infamous for retaliating against her partner's exploitive behavior rather than ignoring or rationalizing it. The beginning and middle parts of Medea's story, however, closely resemble the pattern we have discussed: She is seduced by a flashy guy (Jason the Argonaut), who displays a wide streak of self-interest and duplicity. He exploits her talents for his own gain, and she shows no sign of resisting the exploitation. Eventually, and rather pre-dictably, he betrays her. However, Medea's story has a less than typical ending which may help us expand our view of women and relationships, allowing an open exploration of some seeming contradictions. Let's return to that story now.

CHAPTER THREE

Forging a Partnership

JASON was a prince whose inheritance had been usurped by his uncle Pelias. Pelias had murdered all other heirs to the throne except his brother, Aeson the rightful king, whom he kept in prison and Aeson's son, Jason. At his birth, in order to protect him, Jason's mother had proclaimed him stillborn and sent him away as an infant to Mount Pelion. When he was grown, Jason returned to his homeland and claimed his kingdom. King Pelias told him that before he could have his birthright, he must free his country from a curse by capturing the Golden Fleece.

Sailing on his ship, the *Argo*, Jason and his companions, the Argonauts, come to Colchis in search of the Golden Fleece. In order to win the prize, Jason must accomplish a number of fantastic and seemingly impossible tasks set by Aeetes, the King of Colchis. Jason must harness the fire-breathing, metal-hoofed bulls of Hephaestus, the blacksmith god, to a plow, plow a field with them, and sow the field with serpent's teeth. Fortunately for the Argonauts, the king's daughter, Medea, fell in love with Jason at first sight. Some of the gods who were interested in Jason's cause had persuaded Aphrodite's son, Eros (whom we now call Cupid), to shoot one of his arrows into her heart. Medea, as a sorceress and a priestess of Hecate, knew of a magic lotion which would protect Jason from the bulls. She gave it to him on condition that she would sail with him on the *Argo* as his wife. Medea insisted that Jason swear a holy oath of fidelity to her.

Jason was successful in his labors, but the King of Colchis still did not wish to part with the Golden Fleece and confided his hesitancy to his daughter, Medea. She secretly led Jason to the fleece hanging in the sacred grove behind the palace. Medea enchanted the fierce dragon her father had left to guard the fleece. The Argonauts stole the Golden Fleece and fled on the *Argo* with Medea, pursued by her father's fleet. Medea's half-brother, Apsyrtus, commanded the fleet. Jason and Medea lured him onto an island and murdered him, leaving their pursuers leaderless. Medea and Jason were then purified of the crime of murder by her Aunt Circe, the *Odyssey*'s famous island witch.[1]

The relationship between Jason and Medea is established and maintained by Medea's ability to perform magic. She is indispensable to him because she has knowledge—about her father, about Colchis, about the fleece, about magic—that Jason does not have. He is indispensable to her because she loves him. These initial episodes in the myth are a metaphor for the way in which women tend to use their knowledge about people, emotion, and relationship in order to establish partnerships, particularly romantic and domestic partnerships, often with little or no regard for the authenticity or harmony of the resulting alliance. This is a type of assertion of will that we see women make in many failed partnerships, first willing themselves to achieve an impossible union and then to exact revenge (as we know Medea will) after its failure. What moves women to use their strength and talent in this way?

RELATIONSHIP AS A FEMALE PROVINCE

Women work hard at developing and maintaining connections with others. Intimacy is a both a goal and an ideal. When a woman feels an affinity for someone, she may automatically assume that she should become intimate with that person. When Medea is struck by the arrow of Eros, son of the goddess of love, she has a sudden, dramatic experience of attraction and affinity, an experience that we call "falling in love." Certainly both men and women fall in love. Both men and women may be overwhelmed by the intensity of such an encounter, suffering some diminishment of good judgment as a result. The mythic image of Eros as a capricious, and sometimes malicious, inspirer of love reflects the human experience of a certain kind of passion—sudden, fierce, and inexplicable. Given that such experiences are universal, however, I believe there are some responses to falling in love that are more common in women than in men.

Cora, a successful professional woman with a warm, open personality, talked with me about a hurtful relationship that she stayed in long after its destructive aspects emerged. For Cora, falling in love had produced, as she put it, an "idealized vision of possibilities." This idealized vision had, in a sense, a life of its own. The ideal and the possible were, for a long time, more significant to Cora than the day-to-day reality of the partnership, a day-to-day reality that was actually quite painful. In her words, "I had to dismiss the destructiveness in order to maintain the hope." Having chosen her partner, Cora was prepared "to keep trying, make it better, make it better, fix it." Just like Medea, she did whatever she could, at great cost, to initiate and maintain intimacy with her partner. Like the enchantress of Colchis, Cora had many talents and she put them at the disposal of the relationship and her partner.

This stance toward relationships has been labeled in many ways—codependency being one of the more popular diagnoses. Indeed, it is tempting to pathologize such behavior. When a person appears to be willing to suffer a great deal for little reward and to keep hoping when there is small evidence for hope, are they being anything other than self-destructive? In a word, yes. I think that a woman like Cora is trying to develop identity through relationship. She is trying to discover who she is, to understand her place in the world through the process of forging an intimate partnership. I think, further, that this is a normal process, a normal process that, in relationships like the one she describes, is deformed by a severe imbalance in gender roles. That imbalance causes an association of independence with masculinity and togetherness with femininity. Ideally, both men and women would develop their sense of self through experiences of both intimacy and autonomy, but this rarely seems to happen. Since, like the majority of women, Cora was raised to assume more responsibility for relationships, the asymmetry of the gender roles prompted her to do more than was good for her.

Twenty-five years ago, a researcher named Inge Brover-man and her associates documented this asymmetry when they administered questionnaires to seventy-nine psycho-therapists—a group including psychiatrists, psychologists, and psychiatric social workers.[2] Forty-six of the participants were male and thirty-three were female. The questionnaire was designed to elicit three profiles of a "mature, healthy, socially competent adult." One profile was of the mentally healthy male, one of the healthy female, and the third was of a psychologically healthy human being, not specified as male or female. According to the responding therapists in this study, ideal mental health for a generic human being, not specified by gender, consisted of being independent, com-petitive, aggressive, objective, autonomous, and not easily hurt. Ideal mental health for a man was essentially the same as for the human being. Ideal mental health for a woman was described as being the opposite of good mental health for a human being. Women, if psychologically healthy, should be "more submissive, less independent, less adven-turous, more easily influenced, less aggressive, less com-petitive, [have] their feelings more easily hurt, . . . less objective."[3] These disquieting findings have been supported by many subsequent writers and researchers.

This research delineates American culture's ego ideal and the conventional or typical relationship men and women have to that ideal. By "ego ideal," I mean our collective notion of the model human being. Confirmation of the fact that autonomy, independence, aggression, and invulner-ability are considered the epitome of human development can be found in whom we elect (not someone who cries in public or admits to having been depressed), whom we pay to see at the movies (chiefly action heroes), whom we admire.[4] This image of the ideal person leaves out a number of normal and, in fact, necessary aspects of human experience. There are times in life when dependence is a must, when being hurt or vulnerable is the only realistic response, when aggression and competition are destructive, when objectivity is a sham, and when one must allow oneself to be influenced. How does our culture deal with these inevitable situations, when they run counter to the socially defined ideal? What happens to the normal challenges that cannot be solved or resolved by recourse to the ideal traits? Such situations are split off from our picture of what's important in life and placed in the realm of the feminine. For example, any life event that makes an adult dependent on others—such as illness or old age—takes that person into a world dominated by women. People struggle to be as self-sufficient and independent as they can, to live up to their culture's idea of what constitutes a good adult. When something like an illness makes that struggle impossible, that person goes into a hospital or nursing home and his or her dependency needs are handled, in the vast majority, by women. Women take care of those who cannot care for themselves, who cannot live up to the ideal of autonomy. Our perceptions and assumptions about all of this are normally so automatic and conditioned that we are not aware of "doing" any of it. It feels as if it simply "is."

According to psychologist Jean Baker Miller, "[W]omen, then, become the 'carriers' of those aspects of the total human experience that remain unsolved. . . . These parts of experience have been removed from the arena of full and open interchange and relegated increasingly to a realm outside of full awareness, in which they take on all sorts of frightening attributes."[5] What is meant by calling certain problems "unsolved" in this context? For me, it refers to the way in which pursuit of the ego ideal is held up as a potential panacea. People constantly receive both implicit and explicit instruction to this effect: "the closer to the culture's ego ideal you can get, the happier you will be." In other words, striving to perfect the traits of the ideal within yourself, trying to be more autonomous, competitive, and in control, should solve any problem you have, resolve any issue that comes up. But it doesn't.

Perfecting the traits of the culture's ego ideal does not, for instance, address the problem of connectedness in relationship, the maintenance of togetherness. In fact, an ideal that promotes autonomy and extremes of independence is more likely to produce alienation than intimacy. Miller refers in several different works to the prevalence of alienation as a consistent theme in Western literature and art.[6] Since mainstream literature and art are dominated by men and by men's concerns, she takes this as evidence that alienation is a significant problem for men and attributes this to their position as exemplars of the cultural ideal of independence and autonomy. Because men have historically been permitted to pursue the ego ideal more freely than women, the problematic effects of the ideal, in this case a feeling of alienation, are perhaps more obvious in them.

The pervasiveness of the ideal of perfect autonomy and independence means that connection itself takes place by chance and that ongoing connectedness or togetherness must, if it happens at all, be the province of people who, like women, are closed out of the pursuit of the culture's ego ideal. Thus women are in charge of togetherness. If a woman's class, education, race, or personal persistence make her eligible to go after the ego ideal, and she does so, then she must hire other women to care for her family. These caretakers, by definition and for a variety of involuntary or voluntary reasons, cannot or do not pursue the ideal. Like men without wives to look after the relational part of their lives generally do, a woman who is very devoted to her pursuit of the masculinized ideal often must do without family. Such a woman may well become as alienated as any hero of existential fiction or the hero of any generic Clint Eastwood-style movie.

The ego ideal is sought after by both men and women for the excellent reason that self-esteem is closely associated with it. Considerable psychological research shows that the more masculine traits people (men or women) feel that they have, the better they feel about themselves.[7] Although this is true of both men and women, women are in a particular bind concerning the connection between self-esteem and masculine traits. As the Broverman research tells us, a woman who is healthy as a person is sick as a woman and one who is healthy as a woman is sick as a person.[8] This is the bind that a woman is in when masculinity is the psychological norm; she must choose between the self-esteem of the masculine ego ideal and the richness of pursuing feminine values. If a woman pursues the masculine ego ideal, who will tend to the unsolved problem of connectedness, who will foster togetherness, who will be the keeper of relationship magic, in her personal life and in our society?

What kinds of things happen on the societal level if women are less dedicated to maintaining connectedness?

The latest wave of feminism has produced more opportunity for women (albeit opportunity with a "glass ceiling") and, perhaps more importantly, a clear sense in women that it is appropriate for them to pursue high-status professions. As a result, the two low-status professions that were previously seen as the only suitable choices for women, namely nursing and teaching, no longer benefit from a boundless supply of talented women with no other choices. Nurses and teachers, pursuing vocations in the public sector that require the practice of nurture and care in the context of a personal/professional relationship, have demanded adequate pay and more power. As a result of these changes in women's status and priorities, schools and hospitals, institutions that historically (and unconsciously) depended on a large group of dedicated female employees who would accept marginal pay and problematic conditions, find themselves in financial and organizational crises. If women will not attend to the collective duties of empathy and nurturance for the young and vulnerable members of society, then these devalued and ignored duties go unattended.

But for the most part women still carry these duties, in both the personal and collective spheres. Books and studies like *The Second Shift* document the way in which women simultaneously carry the basic emotional and practical maintenance of home life while also pursuing the higher-status careers now available to them.[9] Consequently, women like Cora are moonlighters, taking on the additional job of working ever harder to create an envisioned togetherness, garnering all of their abilities and concentrating their talents on the relationship on top of their regular work. Women's lives are driven by the motto, "Make it better, make it better, fix it." Cora described her attitude during some of the most difficult periods of her relationship like this: "If I just work at this hard enough, there's no reason why we can't do it." The choice of pronouns is instructive here. If *I* work hard enough, *we* can do it. Like Medea, if I can find the charm, work the magic, I can make the ideal real. It's my job to do this for both of us, for the relationship.

RELATIONSHIP MAGIC

Medea's magic consists of special knowledge, protective spells, and a willingness to relinquish all interests outside her relationship with Jason. It's fairly easy to see the parallel between her special knowledge and women's special knowledge of relationship in our culture; it's easy to see her devotion as a counterpart to female devotion in general. But am I indulging in hyperbole when I compare a woman's talent for relationship to an enchantress's spells? Perhaps not.

Lauren, a woman in her early fifties with a thriving medical practice and a powerful supervisory position in an institution that promotes alternative treatment research, told me about a relationship she had with a man who shared her spiritual values. She had met him while on a religious retreat, and it seemed to her that his world view was much like hers. As an additional benefit, she and her partner shared many interests. This gave them active and compatible leisure time together. The problem? Lauren's partner did not know how to verify his perceptions of others, including Lauren. He was an extreme example of a man who had been taught, by personal history and collective model, to be utterly independent and autonomous in his judgments. And his judgmental perceptions of other people were often destructively off the mark. For example, he might interpret Lauren's way of handing a friend a glass of brandy as an expression of her feelings about that person. He felt that his perception of the meaning of such a gesture was more accurate than Lauren's own sense of her feelings. He and Lauren simply could not come to a meeting of minds over the meaning of many such interpersonal interactions.

Lauren attempted to deal with this through a number of strategies. Being well trained and adept in logical thinking, she first put a great deal of effort into careful explanation, trying desperately to apply rational analysis to her partner's fantasies about her, fantasies that he based on her momentary facial expressions, her menu choices, or chance remarks. She described it like this: "At first I thought it was just a matter of him seeing the light of day. . . . I thought, well, if I just explain to the best of my ability, he'll get it." This strategy failed completely, causing differences to widen.

Lauren developed alternative tactics. "Then I thought for a long time that, if he spends time in the relationship, he will see that I do love and respect him. He'll change. I went through a phase of 'this takes time, he doesn't trust me because his mother was crazy. He has good reason not to trust people, but, as he spends time with me and gets to know me, he'll learn to trust me.' That went on for a few months. I was patient, thinking that he would learn, that present experience would outweigh the past. That was also to no avail. I just kept holding on to the idea that one day he would have a revelation about who I really was. I think I had eternal hope that he would change how he was perceiving me, that what was good in the relationship would overwhelm what was bad." Lauren's final strategy was emotional detachment: "Well, nobody's perfect. . . . My job is to detach, to enjoy the good stuff and ignore the rest."

In developing these creative stratagems, Lauren used both her personal talents and her professional training— her bedside manner in several senses as well as her considerable management experience. She had some fundamental knowledge of interpersonal relationships that her partner simply did not have, and she was completely willing to devote that knowledge to the relationship. More important, the considerable force of Lauren's will and intention was focused on her efforts to foster intimacy and make that intimacy reliable. Like most women, Lauren had been practicing this focus since elementary school. During those latency years (roughly equivalent to elementary school) when children concentrate on competency and skill development, boys typically focus on competition and concrete knowledge, learning how things work. Girls concentrate on the intricacies of human relationships, learning how emotions work, learning how to talk to people. As Carol Gilligan says, "People used to look out on the playground and say that the boys were playing soccer and the girls were doing nothing. But the girls weren't doing nothing—they were talking. They were talking about the world and they became very expert about it, in a way the boys did not."[10] As a consequence, each gender ends up with knowledge that seems secret and occult to the other. Women's knowledge may seem especially occult or magical because it concerns intangibles, namely feelings and relational bonds.

A sorcerer could be defined as one who focuses her full intention and attention on understanding and working with intangible forces, those unseen principles and motivators in life which do not respond to concrete manipulation or rational analysis. To the hyperrational mind-set, a mind-set which is intrinsic to our culture's ego ideal, emotions in general and love in particular are just such intangible forces. To that same mind-set the emotional reality of intimacy may acquire a magical or mystical quality, in part by virtue of being ignored. As Miller says, "These parts of experience [parts classed as feminine, like the work of maintaining intimacy] have been removed from the arena of full and open interchange and relegated increasingly to a realm outside of full awareness, in which they take on all sorts of frightening attributes."[11]

Certain modes of understanding and insight are associated with the feminine and split off into the unconscious. Emotion, intuition, somatic sensation, fantasy, metaphorical association, visualization, and imagination are all sources of perception and knowledge to which women have a special connection, at least in Western culture's collective imagery. Because they are generally classed as irrational, these "ways of knowing" acquire an aura of magic and mystery, even though some are vital to the everyday functioning of intimacy and others are vital to creativity. Mystery, with a feminine cast, surrounds these ways of knowing.

Medea, in the beginning of her story with Jason, is mysterious. The chroniclers take care to let us know that she is a priestess of the goddess Hecate, even though nothing happens that seems to be connected to that fact. Hecate is a mysterious goddess, associated with night, the dark of the moon, with witches, the crossroads, and Cerberus, the three-headed hound that guards the entrance of the underworld. She is an archaic Mistress of the Dark, inclusive of the dark aspects of the Feminine, aspects we often prefer to ignore.[12] As a goddess of patriarchal Greece, Hecate rules the split-off aspects of life that are not attended to by the gods (who might perhaps be seen as early representations of the Western ego ideal). Psychologically, Hecate is an image of the part of self that is comfortable in the unconscious, which pursues intuition and hidden connections outside the light of ego consciousness. As the divine figure who is comfortable at the crossroad between conscious and unconscious knowledge, Hecate is an important mediating figure. To be her priestess, as Medea is, is to be able to mediate between the tangible and the intangible, to negotiate the connection between known and unknown. She knows how to pass in and out of the sacred grove, which signifies her ability to move between the everyday and the otherworldly. She is comfortable handling dragons and magical bulls, while, at the same time, she is a young girl in love who has family problems. Medea is able to live in both the everyday world and Hecate's realm. How is Hecate's realm connected to our discussion of women and relationships? Hecate and her priestess, Medea, indicate the mysterious aura of secret knowledge that femininity has acquired in the Western world.

Returning to Friedan's early work, we find that "the feminine mystique says that the highest value for women is the fulfillment of their own femininity. . . . It says that this femininity is so mysterious and intuitive and close to the creation and origin of life that manmade science may never be able to understand it."[13] In short, it is inexplicable, like magic. Are women intrinsically and essentially priestesses of Hecate, magicians of emotion and connection, or is this view the result of thousands of years of cultural splitting, in which human experience is divided into sets labeled masculine and feminine?

Jungian theorists have incorporated this image of women as holders of a mysterious force of togetherness into their personality theory. Classical Jungian theory postulates an inherent female affinity for Eros, the archetypal principle of relatedness and connection. Jungian analyst Eric Neuman, in his classic work, *Amor and Psyche*, seems to consider that the successful "psychic development of the feminine" depends entirely on the successful union of female consciousness with Eros.[14] In other words, from that point of view a woman's ideal approach to life is based on her ability and desire to foster connection. Is this woman's archetypal nature or simply the projective mantel she carries?

The question of nature versus nurture in regard to the female affinity for Eros to me seems impossible to answer. As mentioned earlier, in Carol Gilligan's recent research we find evidence that girls begin to make an intensive study of the structures of relationship and the function of emotions—these are Eros in action—while in elementary school.[15] The latency-age quest for competency in which boys focus on mechanics and team sports finds little girls focused on connections between people and the unspoken, underlying rules that govern intimacy. When focusing on an area of expertise begins this early, how can one know what is innate? By adulthood these divisions of knowledge function *as if* they were innate. Since the expertise developed by little girls about relationships is considered trivial in relationship to our collective ego ideal (derided, for instance, as gossip), it is generally ignored. However, that expertise is constantly needed in everyday life. The fact that the feminine talent for relationship is simultaneously ignored and in constant use means that girls and women operate in an atmosphere of mystery and, when relating to men, they usually operate unilaterally. By this I mean that it is generally accepted, in an unarticulated way, that women will carry the awareness and exercise the skills that maintain togetherness, and that they will do this automatically and "naturally." The general assumption is that a man will not be actively concerned in the maintenance of a relationship unless a woman demands it.

Let's return for a moment to Lauren's situation. Lauren is a very competent woman who must make difficult professional decisions every day. Yet she could not decide to give up on her relationship. Daily disputes over such minor incidents as the meaning of the way in which she served after-dinner brandy to a friend tore her apart. She responded by practicing relationship magic indiscriminately as she tried to maintain her journey with her partner. Likewise, as Medea continues her journey with Jason, she must come up with strategy after strategy, ploy after ploy, spell after spell to keep the relationship going, to pursue her quest for intimacy. One reason for this seeming desperation might well be that the female partner typically has most of the relationship expertise and therefore feels the primary responsibility for the relationship's maintenance and growth. For Lauren, her strategies worked well enough to keep the relationship going but not well enough to produce genuine intimacy. She felt like a failure, carrying the responsibility for the relationship's functioning. Reflecting on the end of that relationship, Lauren said, "It was after that relationship that

I decided not to be in relationships for a while. I thought 'I need a break.' . . . I thought the break would be at least a year, because this [relationship] was very hard, depressing. It changed how I see people. I think I'm less optimistic now about people changing. I felt completely like a failure." Lauren felt she had failed to protect and preserve her intimate relationship.

THE FEMININE AS REFUGE

Medea's relationship with Jason begins with an act of protection. The story tells us that Medea knew of a magic lotion which would protect Jason from the bulls her father, the King of Colchis, forces Jason to confront.[16] The fierce bulls seem to symbolize aggressive competition; they are a weapon that Medea's father uses in his turf war with Jason. Jason wants something precious, the Golden Fleece, and Aeetes does not want him to have it. Even after Jason is successful in his labors, the King of Colchis does not wish to part with the fleece, and his daughter, Medea, must intervene again. The story does not make it clear to us why the fleece is so precious. The intensity of competition between Jason and the King of Colchis is not explained either.

Theorists in various disciplines have developed explanations for this kind of competition between men. From a Freudian point of view, such competition between men is an outcome of the Oedipal complex, a pivotal childhood conflict that produces intense competitive jealousy between son and father, and by extension between all men. From the point of view of a biological determinist, testosterone and the territorial nature of male primates makes this kind of competition inevitable. From the point of view of conventional wisdom, the motivation for competition might be, "He who dies with the most toys, wins." Although this is a facetious way of expressing it, our culture's ego ideal has enshrined competition as an intrinsically wholesome and beneficial form of human interaction, essential to success.

In a social setting that associates self-esteem with competition, aggression, and hyperrationality, people have desperate need of a refuge. Normal needs and vulnerabilities cannot be openly dealt with in such a cutthroat setting and must be handled outside mainstream discourse. The need to grieve, be comforted, relax, be silly, or simply be still has no legitimate part in the marketplace or in the creed of total self-sufficiency.

More subtly, an atmosphere of relentless striving, concrete pragmatism, and objectivity gives rise to a feeling of emptiness and alienation. The philosopher Max Weber referred to this feeling as "disenchantment" and saw it as the inevitable outcome of hyperrationality and intellectualization. The result, according to Weber, is that "the ultimate, the most sublime values have withdrawn from public life either into the transcendental realm of mysticism or into . . . personal relationships.[17] Jessica Benjamin, a feminist psychoanalyst building on Weber's insight, defines disenchantment as the "impersonality and neutrality bred by rationalization." She goes on to address disenchantment as a gender issue. Because hyperrationality mirrors our image of masculinity and represses those values we class as feminine, the disenchantment associated with the dominance of rational ways of knowing is identified with masculine values. The reenchantment of life is associated with the reclamation of feminine values. Benjamin is particularly concerned with the way in which this search for reenchantment places pressure on individual mothers to create a special private sphere of connectedness and nurturance which will save themselves and their families from the emptiness of a disenchanted world. Disenchantment "inevitably stimulates the search for reenchantment [through the search] . . . for a regendered version of society."[18]

In the search for reenchantment, women and their spheres of influence, i.e., intimacy and domestic life, are imagined as a sanctuary from the strain and feelings of emptiness that are an inevitable byproduct of the pursuit of the masculinized ego ideal. Just as Medea provides a protective potion that shields Jason from the king's aggressive attempts to stymie or destroy him, women strive to provide a shelter for their loved ones. The appeal that Martin Heidegger made to Hannah Arendt, like the one that the wizard makes in the beginning of "Fitcher's Bird"—a plea for special understanding and help—is a powerful one to women. They feel a responsibility to provide a shelter in the home. A sheltering home life is not typically seen as the outcome of mutual efforts from all family members, nor is it understood as a difficult feat given the culture's dominant values. The refuge of intimacy, hominess, and feeling is pictured as the outcome of a woman's love. The predominant attitude is that it should be easily (even if somewhat mysteriously) within a woman's power to provide the relationship magic needed for an intimate sanctuary.

Yet, ironically, values and activities that are outside the culture's ego ideal, that are classed as feminine and used to maintain intimacy, are seen as trivial, simplistic, and mysterious, in a minor way. This has something to do with the feelings of failure that women often have about their relationships. It should all come easily, an outgrowth of womanly love. As Lauren said, "I felt completely like a failure. [I was] trying to make this better all the time and it got worse, no matter what I did to make it better." People seem to feel that women have a special service to give, a protective service like Medea's to Jason when she shielded him from the bulls, making it possible for him to proceed with his quest.

THE BEGINNING OF THE FEMALE QUEST FOR INTIMACY

The saga of the Golden Fleece is Jason's heroic quest. In the mythic motif of a quest, the hero is called to take a perilous journey, to attain the unattainable, to find something ineffably precious and bring it back. Such a quest is, in the psychological sense, a search for that which is missing from consciousness, here symbolized by the mysterious Golden Fleece. Many have explored this ancient and widespread story form from the point of view of the (usually) male hero. Joseph Campbell's book *Hero with a Thousand Faces* is probably the best known and most influential study of the hero's quest. He sees the heroic quest as a "monomyth," the structure underlying all myths and folklore. Campbell uses Jung's theory of individuation to interpret the questing journey as a metaphor for the ego's journey through the unconscious, seeking union with the transpersonal aspect of the self. The transpersonal aspect of the self is represented in the questing tale by the sought after object, the Holy Grail, the Golden Fleece. In this framework of interpretation, a woman often appears to facilitate the hero's encounter with the goddess, the primal feminine.[19] Medea is that woman in Jason's quest.

But what happens if we make Medea the protagonist of

the story? If Medea is, in our interpretation, no longer a symbol of something the hero needs to deal with but is, instead, engaged in a quest of her own, what is she questing for? In overarching psychological terms, the female quest for intimacy is a quest for individuation, for the manifestation of the self, just as the heroic quest is in Campbell's analysis. However, individuation, which is the development and expression of the authentic self over the course of a lifetime, is different for women than for men. Consequently, the female quest has its own unique qualities.

To more fully understand those unique qualities let's look at some psychological, social, and physiological conditions of womanhood that influence individuation. Psychologically, most women develop with a more complex "inner world" than most men. To understand the inner world of women we must understand the unique way in which a typical girl develops, psychologically, in our culture. As psychologist Nancy Chodorow[20] and others have explored childhood development, a picture emerges that is very different than the old psychological model, which held up male development as the norm. In the old model, female development was presented as incomplete male development. However, a new model of women's normal psychological development, from childhood to old age, gives clues to what women are seeking in their search for meaningful relationships.

In normal early development, a child experiences her parents as part of herself, and the internalization of her parents' attitudes has great power to form and organize her emerging personality. Children typically express themselves freely. Their authentic or genuine traits are very close to the surface. Parents' reactions to the child's expressions of her true self become the core of the child's own attitude toward herself. The child builds a cohesive sense of who she is out of the dynamic interaction between her innate potential and the responses she receives from important people in her world, her parents being the most influential. Those parts of the self that are acceptable to the family are developed and supported; those that the family cannot recognize or accept are, at the least, neglected. Parts of the child's self that are especially challenging to her parents will be more actively suppressed and repressed, often becoming a source of shame for the child. In this way the expression of, and even the awareness of, the authentic self is modified by the child's internalization of the attitudes and reactions she experiences with important adults. The adults' assumptions about gender are passed on to the child and influence the development of the child's innate qualities.

Consequently, there are significant gender differences in the process of ongoing internalization and self-discovery. Boys are generally encouraged, at about school age, to separate rather definitively from their mothers. If they do not, they risk being labeled a "baby," a "mama's boy" or a "sissy"—the most awful things to be in our masculine culture. Typically boys then embark on a lifelong quest to become their fathers' equal competitor and eventual replacement. This is a kind of bond to the father, but not exactly an intimate bond. In order to develop a culturally appropriate masculine gender role, a boy pursues the relatively simple, if harsh, path of cutting off his sense of oneness with his mother and taking a competitive stance toward both his father and any siblings he may have. The development of a culturally appropriate feminine gender role requires a girl to maintain a close, empathetic, noncompetitive attunement with many different family members, however complex and conflicted the demands of those different relationships might be.

These early experiences leave women with a complex, interwoven set of relationship patterns. The developmental strategy of the male gender role—that of renouncing one's similarities with the opposite-sex parent and competitively striving to be like the same-sex parent—is not available to girls. Girls need to stay identified with their mothers while forming an intimate bond with their fathers. At the same time, a girl must not interfere with the bond between her mother and father, and if she is to conform to the feminine gender role, she needs to maintain nurturing, noncompetitive bonds with any siblings there may be in the family. This situation requires a girl child to stay open and receptive to a number of styles of relationship and a number of ways of being in relationships. The efforts a girl makes to be successfully intimate in all of these very different relationships requires her to move freely back and forth between the often contradictory outer behaviors and inner feelings that make each connection possible. She strives to stay "at one" with her mother without competing with her, to also identify with her father (while still trying to be appropriately feminine), and to take a caring "little mother" stance toward siblings who may be depriving her of parental attention, while still trying to get her own childish needs met. Meanwhile, the demands placed on developing boys are to strive for competency rather than closeness and to identify in a competitive way with father, but with no one else in the family.

Inevitably, the nature of a girl's early relationships impacts the way she develops. A girl must have a sense of self that allows for these multiple connections, a sense of self that allows her to handle the contradictory feelings involved. The sense of self that allows for this centers around a core experience of "I am a person who loves and cares for these other people." That core enables a girl and an adult woman to comfortably attune herself to the changing needs involved in varying situations and relationships. Identity constellates around the ability to connect with people and foster closeness. Internal and external boundaries must be malleable for girls and women if they are to achieve this in the majority of their relationships, certainly more malleable than the strict interpersonal or intrapsychic boundaries pictured in the cultural ego ideal. For that ego ideal, the self is free-standing, not dependent on others for definition, and takes its individuality from a set of consistent traits that do not change from situation to situation.

A woman's inner world, with its multiple paths and apparent contradictions, is not mirrored in the typical images of American culture. Our popular images tend to reflect striving and autonomy, the Hero's journey, not interconnection and multiplicity of being. The ideal male psyche, as reflected in Broverman's research, is reflected in America's portraits of ideal people. The female psyche has few, if any, positive representations. Flexible boundaries are presented, in story and instruction, as pathological. The multifaceted reality of a woman's inner life finds almost no mirror in culture. I think that the female quest for intimacy has something to do with bringing this inner world into relationship to the outer world, to manifest this layered internal experience in external life through a primary partnership and the creation of a new family.

Cora describes the beginning of her quest like this: "I envisioned an ideal. It was an ideal I had pictured for a long time, and had pursued in other relationships, but it was activated with this person in a new way. This was the first time that the partnership I wanted seemed possible in terms of who my partner was—I had left my marriage because of my belief that my husband lacked the ability to create a partnership like the one I imagined." Cora went on to explain that she was not envisioning a perfect man but a type of relationship which would allow her to become more completely herself and do the same for her partner. This internal image, so vital to Cora's sense of herself, was nowhere reflected in her culture. She imagined building it within the protected confines of a romantic partnership.

Cora was living day to day in one reality and imagining, at the same time, that she could create a different reality. This happens because women live both in the dominant culture and in a "muted" female culture that is not fully conscious even to themselves.[21] A twofold awareness is necessary to social survival for women. This is one of the social conditions of womanhood that impact the quest for intimacy. On one level, a woman's double consciousness requires an awareness of the acknowledged, dominant social reality and the confined role a woman is assigned in it. This awareness coexists, on another level, with an acute comprehension of an ignored reality, the female reality which is edited out of the cultural ideal. This concept echoes W. E. B. Dubois's notion of "double consciousness" in African Americans.[22]

This twofold awareness becomes increasingly layered for

most girls and women. They live intimately with fathers, brothers, lovers, husbands, and sons—males who embody, however partially, the values of the dominant culture. If a woman is heterosexual, her most powerful personal emotions may be invested in relationships that require the fullest repression of the unacknowledged parts of her experience. The double consciousness of women is replete with contradictory feelings of attachment and resentment toward men.

This contributes to the complexity of the inner world of women, most of whom consciously adhere to their culture's ideal while experiencing a shadow, or muted, culture of their own. The existence of a muted female culture is one reason that the simple act of a group of women telling each other their stories can be experienced by them as revolutionary (these were once called consciousness-raising groups). The muted culture is being explicated, brought out from the shadow, in such a group. Images and stories from the old goddess cultures may also owe some of their contemporary popularity to the fact that they reflect a complex, interwoven view of the world that mirrors the layered consciousness of women.

The physiological reality of female sexual experience may also contribute to the manifold nature of the female internal world. Many feminist theorists think that the physical experiences of penetrability and menstruation, the ability to experience multiple orgasm, to give birth and breast-feed, mean that women must experience the self and the world as cyclical, interpenetrated, and unboundaried.[23] I am in a quandary about these ideas. It seems to me that the specific nature of one's body must affect one's experience of the world, as well as one's psychological state, and that this must contribute to the gender differences we find in attitudes toward intimacy. Jung states categorically that the body is the ground and source of all archetypal experience.[24] At the same time, biology is not destiny, and the belief that it is serves as a rationale for oppressive social constrictions. It seems to me that the fundamental nature of our bodies forms the basis of our experience, but, at the same time, our sex does not define the limits of our possibilities.

When I asked Cora if there were moments in her failed relationship when her ideal was realized, she said, "You mean, did it become flesh?" This is the image that inspires the female quest for intimacy, the image of a complex inner world made flesh in partnership. Given that straight as well as gay women seem to find it easier to be fully understood and recognized by other women, why do straight women continue to pursue this quest with men? Is this simply a by-product of heterosexual orientation? Men are encouraged to embody the cultural ego ideal and to focus on the outside world almost exclusively. This means that a woman might see a man as her connection to the outside world. As psycho-analyst Jessica Benjamin puts it, "To find another path to the world they [women] often look for a man whose will they imagine to be untrammeled."[25] In fantasy, such a man can make the ideal real. The hope is that a partnership with him will have a mediating effect on the split the woman experiences between her inner reality and the outer world, that it will foster a viable connection between muted feminine culture and dominant culture. This may be the hope that someone like Hannah Arendt has when she becomes involved with a charismatic, problematic man—the hope that such a man can provide a path between inner and outer life. When a woman says, as Lauren did, "I just kept holding on to the idea that one day he would have a revelation about who I really was," she is talking about being recognized by her beloved, something both men and women long for. But she is also talking about the hope that her relationship with a particular man will bring "who she really is" into the world.

Our partnerships in life help us negotiate and work through the interface between our unique, authentic selves and conventional society. When the intimate partnership is between a man and a woman, this negotiation is complicated and skewed by the fact that men and women have come to inhabit such disparate emotional worlds—Venus and Mars, according to one popular author[26]—and by the fact that the masculine emotional world is endorsed by society as the norm. As a consequence, women experience a much greater distance between authentic self and conventional society than most men seem to. Because of this skew, women may also experience a particular need for masculine help in working through a satisfying interface between the self and society's expectations.

According to classical Jungian theory, a woman develops her authentic self, in part, through developing a relationship to an aspect of her psyche called the "animus." The animus is "the inner man who acts as a bridge between the woman's ego and her own creative resources."[27] The ego is the conscious sense of self, of identity. The inner man embodies undeveloped parts of the self that are experienced as masculine. For many women these untapped resources are what they need to make a place for themselves in the world. Jason could be seen, symbolically, as Medea's animus, and their marriage could represent the internal joining of masculine and feminine parts of the self. Jason does prompt Medea to develop her creative resources and he does connect her to the outside world. But because the union of Jason and Medea is, ultimately, such a spectacular failure, I am going to treat it as a metaphor for the way in which the development of the animus is sometimes distorted. Again and again, we see women depending on an external partner for this development, projecting the power of the animus onto their spouses. These women appear to be separated from the animus as an internal experience. Instead of developing their own creative resources, they seek them in a partner.

SEPARATION FROM THE ANIMUS

When Medea helps Jason murder her half-brother, Apsyrtus, she has reached a turning point in her journey. Her allegiance has moved, completely and beyond the possibility of a change of heart, from her family to Jason. What sort of psychological turning point might this symbolize? I think that, in a certain kind of intimate relationship, a woman may abandon the internal development of the animus. Here Medea's animus is symbolized by her half-brother, who is both like and unlike Medea, part of her genetic inheritance and part "other." She destroys him to further her connection to Jason. This is a metaphor for her abandonment of the internal development of her animus as an aspect of herself and her projection of it onto Jason. Such a projection is a psychological displacement in which the power of the animus is shifted from within the self, to an external relationship, in this case with Jason. When the animus's power to connect a woman to her creative resources is projected onto a man, that man's opinion of the woman becomes extremely potent, perhaps more potent than her own opinion.

Cora described many experiences in which her partner's remarks, sometimes pointed, sometimes offhand, had the power to define her own view of herself. He would comment on her style of problem solving, and she would begin to wonder if she could rely on it. She described it this way: "Those comments pierced me. I would struggle with them, and, if it seemed they had any validity, they would lodge in me." Even at the time of our conversation, many years after Cora had broken off this relationship, she struggled with some of those remarks. The power to assess herself had been given over to her partner. Her view of the most undeveloped and vulnerable aspects of herself was deeply affected in this relationship and, as a consequence, the way she did or did not express those aspects of herself was changed. She was projecting one of the primary functions of the animus onto her partner, the function of noticing and knowing the parts of herself that were not yet fully recognized.

The concept of the animus is controversial, particularly among feminists. A major difficulty with Jung's theory comes from his portrayal of the animus as an embodiment of stereotypical masculine traits, such as assertiveness, rationality, control, and abstraction. He presented the animus as the embodiment of eternal, universal, and archetypal masculinity.[28] Jung showed little awareness of the impact of culture on the construction of gender traits. Consequently his theory came to resemble a form of biological determinism, with all of that notion's oppressive history and potential. Jung's usual definition of the animus closely resembles the Broverman profile of the psychologically healthy adult (male), that assemblage of traits I have been calling the American culture's ego ideal.

Many efforts have been made by post-Jungian writers to disentangle the concept of the animus from these problematic issues. They have expended this intellectual effort in part because animus figures continue to take significant roles in women's dreams and fantasies. This simply means that women dream about and imagine male figures whose role is to help the woman develop parts of herself that are longing for expression. The key to what is still useful to women about the concept of the animus lies in this function of making a bridge between a woman's notion of who she is and her undeveloped potentials, especially those potentials that don't fit perfectly with the woman's current self-image. Masculine images representing these undeveloped parts of the self may come up in the imagination because a male figure is the most different from the female ego's picture of itself.

I once knew a woman artist who dreamed constantly of a bull. The bull represented her most radical artistic vision. The maleness of this symbol was vital to her relationship with this undeveloped part of herself. The bull's macho forcefulness was both frightening and invigorating to the artist. She began to imagine ways in which she might relate to the bull—would she find it a mate? would she become a bullfighter?—and this allowed her to work around the difficulty she was having in accepting the intensity of her artistic vision. In working with this image, she was making a conscious relationship with a primal animus figure and, in the process, tapping into her hidden or denied potential. The nature and development of the animus as an internal phenomenon is vital to this ongoing dialogue between the ego's idea of who we are and the potentials within the self that constantly bubble up. Will the ego have an adversarial relationship to parts of the self which are very different from itself? Will it be curious about these deep potentials? Disgusted? Frightened? Elated?

The animus is the aspect of the psyche that fosters and embodies the capacity to relate to differences within, to make bridges with the parts of the self that are the most unlike the conscious ego. The animus carries out a function of "portraying alternatives," of presenting the ego with ways of seeing and doing things that diverge from its habitual ways.[29] For women whose sense of self has been deeply affected by the patriarchal definition of femininity, masculine symbolic figures, like the bull in the dreams of the artist, may be especially necessary to embody parts of the self which, in that patriarchal view, are distinctly unfeminine. Positive animus figures, like the bull in the dreams of the artist, may provide a feeling of approval or security when such a woman is defying convention by developing those parts of the self.

Because animus figures are internal, usually unconscious parts of the self that begin to take shape in childhood, their specific character is greatly affected by important male figures in childhood. For instance, a father who is uninterested in or perhaps very critical of his daughter may be internalized as a disinterested or hypercritical relationship between the ego and other parts of the self. When in adulthood a woman projects animus figures onto external people (usually men), she experiences these undeveloped parts of herself as being part of the other person or as being in the charge of the other person. For example, Cora began to depend on her partner to oversee her attempts to problem-solve, because she projected this ability onto him. Her ego did not recognize and develop this capacity within herself but recognized it only in her partner. Projection is a process in which an unconscious quality or potential is perceived in an outer object or person, rather than in the self. Jung sees some projection as inevitable, even useful in that, if the projection is noticed, it can facilitate an increase in the projector's self-knowledge.[30] In order for such a projection to be useful, it must be recognized as a projection and acknowledged by the projector, who can then take on responsibility for consciously developing that part of the self. So, when Cora realized that she was projecting the ability to solve problems onto her partner, this prompted her to try to understand her distrust of her own ability and to begin to rely on herself. Ideally the relationship which had held and fostered the projection would then continue on a more realistic basis.

However, when a woman projects onto a partner the power to mediate between parts of her self, she takes a number of risks. The foremost risk is that the projection will become entrenched in the relationship. In other words, the power of the animus complex is continuously felt as a real power belonging to the partner. The woman who is projecting her animus onto a man is projecting parts of the self of which she is unconscious but which she needs.[31] For individuation to continue she must, over time, become conscious of these parts. But what if the relationship is set up in such a way that she cannot or will not relate to these projected traits as parts of herself? What does this mean in regard to the particular animus trait I've discussed, the ability to mediate between disparate parts of the self and make a place for the authentic self in the world? The partner acquires the power to deeply affect, perhaps even determine, what the woman feels she can do and be. He acquires tremendous influence over her connection between her inner world and the outer world. When, after World War II, Hannah Arendt accepted Heidegger's opinion of the past and valued it over her own, perhaps something like this was happening. Her ability to protect herself from exploitation and see things clearly was seriously undermined when she substituted his perceptions for hers.

Cora described the way in which her perceptions were affected by her separation from her own animus function, in that she tended to ignore certain things: "It was a question of knowing but not letting myself know." I was intrigued by this remark, particularly since Cora was not the only woman I had heard say something like this. Psychologists have a variety of names for the ways in which people prevent themselves from consciously acknowledging something they actually know. But in simply labeling or pathologizing this response, we ignore its pervasiveness, its "normalcy," if we define normal as customary or typical. Women frequently put aside what they notice, what they know on a gut level, and accept in its place a received opinion, a construct about the relationship they are living. The power to delineate reality, to decide what is important, seems to be handed over to the partner or to the ideal vision of the relationship or both. This is a key finding of Gilligan's research: girls, at the onset of puberty, begin to abandon their own perceptions. "As the phrase 'I don't know' enters our interviews with girls at this developmental juncture, we observe girls struggling over speaking and not speaking, knowing and not knowing, feeling and not feeling, and we see the makings of an inner division. We saw this struggle affect their feelings about themselves, their relationships with others, and their ability to act in the world."[32]

When Cora makes a statement like, "I ignored what was hurting me, things I already knew but I couldn't let be real because that would lead to action," she is describing her heroic efforts to preserve intimacy by maintaining an inner division of the kind that Gilligan notices developing in girls at puberty. In order to continue questing for the ideal relationship she envisioned, she was willing to ignore her discomfort, to put it outside her perception of the relationship, just as the women courted by Bluebeard put aside their well-founded doubts. In this way, self-protection is subverted and becomes relationship-protection instead, acting out a split we have noticed in other areas, the split between self and relationship. In order to be able to do this, a woman must be detached from certain aspects of the animus, most prominently the willingness to rely on one's own perceptions and the power to be fierce in one's own protection. A curious feature of Medea's story is that she is so powerful, particularly in these initial episodes, but still begins to give herself away. Cora and Lauren are strong, competent, effective, thoughtful women who gave themselves away in intimate relationships. The same could be said of Hannah Arendt. If we continue to explore the nature of Medea's power, her relationship magic, we may gain further insight into this conundrum of the powerful woman who loses herself in a relationship.

Medea gives Jason the benefit of all of her knowledge, then she abandons her life and her family so she can sail with him on the *Argo* as his wife. She demands that Jason swear a holy oath of fidelity to her. In this, Medea makes explicit a contract that is sometimes left unspoken: "I will sacrifice myself to this relationship in return for constancy." This could be understood as the result of excessive dependency, or it could be seen as Medea's effort to secure the needed conditions for her quest. A fundamental condition necessary for the quest for intimacy is continuity of relationship. Continuity in relationship is necessary for working with projections, such as the animus projections we have been discussing. Working through projections is vital to the process of manifesting the inner world, "making it flesh" through partnership. Jung saw the process of projection as a natural part of individuation, one of the ways in which relationships help us know ourselves. When we project undeveloped parts of the self onto a partner, we create an opportunity. The opportunity is to notice the projection and in that way become conscious of the part of the self that is projected. This process takes time.

"Individuation" is a Jungian term for the development, over a lifetime, of the unique self. Jung's original work on marriage as a psychological relationship suggests there is a dichotomy between marriages in which the partners expect the marriage to solve life's problems and a marriage, presumably more mature, in which partners realize that solutions only lie within themselves.[33] Thus Jung supports the idea, commonly held in our culture, that development of self and development of relationships are mutually exclusive. A theorist named Adolph Guggenbühl-Craig has taken issue with this dichotomy of personal vs. interpersonal development. He proposes a different view of the purpose of marriage. He believes that, with sufficient consciousness and willingness on the part of each partner to accept the uniqueness of the other, vital relationships between aspects of the self may be worked out through the interpersonal adaptations which are necessary to ongoing, committed intimacy.[34]

Individuation is a movement toward wholeness powered by the integration of conscious and unconscious parts of the personality. As Jungian analyst Andrew Samuels puts it, "This suggests becoming oneself, the person one was intended to be, achieving one's potential. That implies a recognition and acceptance of parts of oneself that are initially repugnant or seem negative, and also an opening up towards the possibilities presented by . . . the animus (or anima in the man), which can act as a gateway or guide to the unconscious. This integration leads not only to a greater degree of self-realization but also to the awareness that one has a self."[35] Some think of individuation as the "making up of the soul,"[36] a process that is not simply about the personality but about spiritual meaning. How is this a part of intimate relationships?

When Cora envisions her ideal relationship, when she imagines the way she could develop her potential within that ideal, she is talking about more than career, contentment, life goals, and retirement plans. She is trying to develop meaning in her life through her relationship. When Lauren talks about her passionate desire that her partner realize who she really is, she is talking about all of who she is, tangible and intangible, pragmatic parts and soulful aspects. These women are hoping to discover, develop, and find a home for all of the self, to individuate through intimacy.

The ways in which individuation is normally pictured show the bias toward excessive autonomy that is common to Western culture. Guggenbühl-Craig notes the autism of most descriptions of individuation and suggests, as a counterpoint, that the dialectic in marriage is a special path for the development of the soul. Guggenbühl-Craig discusses an important difference in purposes for intimate relationships, the difference between well-being and salvation. Well-being as a goal might include material security, physical health, and contentment. To authentically pursue life's meaning and the development of the soul in a partnership, i.e., to frame salvation as the relationship's purpose, may contradict well-being since pursuing salvation and meaning will inevitably involve conflict and suffering.[37]

In our secular culture, the soul has become an abstract notion, an idea that seems to have to do with good values, ethical behavior, and, perhaps, something about identity, something about "who you really are." In Jungian psychology, the experience of the soul is the experience of meaning. When something feels very meaningful, the soul is awakened. These experiences are not intellectual or abstract, but *felt*. The soul must be carried and nurtured in life. A person's best hopes, highest sense of purpose, and her sense of connectedness to life's meaning are the expressions of the soul, and the soul must have a home in the everyday. Historically, the various established religions have served this purpose, providing a home for the soul. The images, rituals, and rules of religion helped people picture and live on the soul's level. These religious institutions have, for very many contemporary Americans, lost the power to do this. For many people, sex and relationships have become the place where they work out the meaning and purpose of their lives. For others money and power seem to serve this function, but that is another book. The soul must be carried by something in daily life and often that something is the beloved.

When the soul is developed through relationship, according to Guggenbühl-Craig, "Partners in the interpersonal relationship function for each other as intrapsychic opposites to be reconciled in individuation."[38] In other words, the development of the soul is projected onto the partner and onto one's relationship with the partner. For this to work successfully, both partners must have great tolerance for the character and behavior of the other. The partners must fully confront one another and engage wholeheartedly in intimacy in order for individuation, rather than simply stagnant projection, to result. Constancy and presence, and fidelity to the primacy of the relationship, are fundamental to the effort. This, in effect, was what Medea was asking of Jason when she asked him to take an oath of fidelity. It simply takes time to bring the potentials to consciousness, to work through the projections. Given all that we have discussed, it seems that the female quest for intimacy is closely related to the path of individuation that Guggenbühl-Craig suggests. Many women seem to be seeking salvation—that is, meaning and authentic individuation—through intimacy. An oath of fidelity, if held, would provide the secure ground that is needed for a mutual process of discovery and individuation.

In this initial inquiry into Medea's story, we have

sketched out the beginning of the female quest for intimacy as well as some of that quest's purposes, stages, and hazards. Women use their focused intention and skill to try to establish an intimate relationship which will function as a refuge. Within that refuge, a woman "opens herself to the possibility of a relationship which will . . . allow her to be the woman she wants to be."[39] Within the container of the ongoing relationship, women hope (sometimes consciously, sometimes unconsciously) to manifest and develop an inner world which is not reflected in the culture at large and also to foster their partner's development. They frequently pursue this goal without considering fundamental issues of compatibility. This reflects both the heroic passion of the quest and the imbalance of gender roles, an imbalance that gives women an inordinate amount of responsibility for intimacy. The imbalance of gender roles also encourages women to neglect inner work on the animus and adds to the difficulty of working on animus projections. The woman's quest for intimacy is a quest to develop the soul in a particular path, a path which may be counter to well-being but is aimed toward salvation through relationship. This means that the unfolding of the relationship is meant to provide authentic meaning, purpose, and depth to the woman's life, not simply to provide concrete well-being.

Just as all heroes on quests tolerate danger and discomfort in order to achieve their goal, women are willing to tolerate considerable suffering in order to achieve intimacy. In many cases, a woman engaged in this quest may also suffer from a lack of confidence or self-esteem and this will increase her willingness to tolerate a destructive partner. However, in the grip of the archetypal power of a quest, the partner's dangerous attributes may seem like the dragon guarding the fleece—something to be lulled and gotten around. The magical aura that surrounds female relationship skills supports the fantasy held by many men and women that any man, even a demonstrable Bluebeard, is really a fairy-tale Beast who can be transformed by a loving, determined Beauty. This belief is illustrated in Medea's story by her belief that an adventurer like Jason can be transformed by an oath of marital fidelity. A further dimension to this fantasy is the belief that this hoped-for transformation of the man and the relationship, if achieved, would be a home for something vital in the woman, something undeveloped and, as a consequence, unknown. It would be a home where both woman and man could become their truest selves.

CHAPTER FOUR

Making a Home in a Disenchanted World

MEDEA carried with her the fabulous Cauldron of Regeneration. Dismembered animals and people were stewed in it and reborn with new power and vigor. After filling the teeming vessel with secret elements, "She mixed the whole concoction thoroughly, stirring it with a long withered branch . . . suddenly, as she moved the old stick round and round in the bowl of hot liquid, the branch grew green, clothed itself in leaves and, an instant later, was laden with heavy clusters of olives. Whenever the heat of the fire caused the froth to boil over out of the bronze cauldron, so that warm drops fell on the earth, the ground at that point grew green and flowers and soft grass sprang up." When they returned to Jason's homeland, Medea used her Cauldron of Regeneration to revitalize old Aeson, Jason's father, by dismembering him and submerging him in the boiling potion. "Quickly his hair and beard lost their whiteness, turning dark once more. The shriveled, neglected look of old age vanished. New flesh filled out his sagging wrinkles, and his limbs grew young and strong. The old man marveled at the change in himself, this was the Aeson of forty years ago."[1] When Medea and Jason returned to Pelias's court with the Golden Fleece, Medea demonstrated her magic to Pelias and his daughters by cutting up an old sheep and cooking it in the cauldron. Out sprang a new lamb. When she offered to renew the youth of Pelias, Jason's old uncle who had usurped Jason's throne, Pelias's daughters dismembered him willingly. However, Medea refused to complete the spell and Pelias was not reborn. In this way, Jason avenged his uncle's betrayal of his father and himself.

The image of Medea's cauldron is in many ways disagreeable: its processes are messy, bloody, frightening, and upsetting. The cauldron is an image of visceral reality; it is a vessel that holds the elemental power of nature. The cycle of disintegration and regeneration is messy and disturbing; the Cauldron of Regeneration aptly represents this. Possessing the cauldron marks Medea as a priestess of nature, an adept of natural forces. Just as dismemberment precedes regeneration in the cauldron, nature renews life by taking life apart. The fundamental regeneration of life depends on the disintegration of life. Organic decay produces fertile soil. A plant must die and go to seed in order for new plants to grow.

In Medea's cauldron, the dismembered are reborn, made whole, and given vitality. The symbol of the cauldron has persisted through the centuries. Over time, this powerful vessel became associated with the witches' cauldron. In the Western world this aspect of nature, its cycles of destruction and rebirth, is seen only in its shadow form, something to be feared and vilified. Females who are associated with these primordial forces are dangerous hags with evil intent, they are the personification of nature at its worst: destructive, devouring, out of control.

The mystique that surrounds women as experts in the interrelated domains of emotion, vulnerability, and relationship is part of a larger bundle of associations. These associations categorize the feminine with nature as a whole. Consequently, the feminine as a whole and women as individuals partake of the profoundly mixed feelings that Western culture has about nature, feelings that range from idealization to terror and contempt. The typical image of the witch pictures the connection between women and nature in a way that expresses negative feelings about both. As a practitioner of relationship magic, a woman is always in danger of being seen, by herself and by others, as a witch. If she is able to maintain smooth relationships in which everyone is comfortable, her efforts and skill in maintaining intimacy are glossed over, veiled in feminine mystique. A successful refuge of intimacy, hominess, and feeling is pictured as the simple outcome of a woman's love. From this perspective, a woman should easily (even if somewhat mysteriously) be able to provide the relationship magic needed for an intimate sanctuary, a real home. Even if she is not able to produce good relationships, she is still seen, by herself and others, as having the power to do so. If relationships are not working out, the woman is responsible: she is messing up, or worse, purposely causing pain. She becomes an evil relationship magician—a witch. The distance between the positive mystique of the good relational woman and the negative mystique of the witch can be quickly traversed.

The Cauldron of Regeneration symbolizes cyclical processes in which one state flows into another; the cauldron destroys and revitalizes, disconnects and connects, dismembers and remembers. It is both a ghoulish brew and a divine elixir. Light and shadow are not divided in this ancient image.[2] In contemporary Western culture, the witch inherited Medea's cauldron. Think of Macbeth's encounter with the three weird sisters, who are cooking up his downfall in their black pot on the blasted heath; or consider Hansel and Gretel's woodland witch, who hopes to cook them up. The witches of the Western world may have Medea's cauldron, but somehow it no longer regenerates. It only destroys.

The witch with her cauldron is a female shadow carrier in the symbolic realm of the imagination. The popular and persistent iconography of the witch probably springs from a primordial world view that persisted into the Christian era, combined with the Church's projections of shadow material onto women. Witches are close to animals and nature. They can shapeshift, fly, go from old to young and back again. They influence feelings, thoughts, relationships, bodies. These images of witches and witchcraft are ancient metaphors of transformation, rooted in prehistoric shamanic practices. Shamans had ecstatic experiences that were grounded in narratives of dismemberment and rebirth. The use of talismans, the ability to affect the course of natural events and interactions with fantastic animals are all common in reports of shamanic journeys. These experiences portray an intimacy with nature. We can see examples of all of them in Medea's story. The Golden Fleece is a talisman, Medea is able to effect the natural course of aging, and she is comfortable with dragons. Medea seems to practice a shamanic form of magic, and this is the main way in which she is historically connected to the witches who emerge in later centuries.

Carlo Ginzburg, an Italian historian, finds considerable evidence in transcripts of witch trials that many who were tried as witches used remnants of old shamanic ritual to produce visionary trances and connect to nature. Members of these cults followed underworld goddesses who lived in the realm of the dead but whose effect on earth was beneficial, particularly in the decay-renewal cycle of agriculture. Ginzburg traces the way in which, over time, the Church inquisitors demonized both the shamanic rituals and the goddess figures that characterized this form of spiritual experience. Church functionaries actively introduced the notions of devil worship, sexual perversion, and infant cannibalism into the testimony of people involved in these rites and cults. Thus the clergy's projections about witchcraft and evil were laid over the vestiges of an ancient nature worship, eventually producing our picture of witches and their sabbaths.[3]

The Cauldron of Regeneration and its mistress, Medea, give us a paradoxical image, an image that combines the power to unite with the power to destroy. This is a prime metaphor for the real nature of Eros. As in Medea's cauldron, emotions in intimate relationships go through rounds of decay and rebirth, reflecting the rhythm and mystery of nature. As with the cauldron, some cycles lead to death and some to renewal. The power of Eros can, through love, replenish a relationship which has withered or, as we have seen in both Cora and Lauren's stories, great power and effort can be expended on a relationship that repeatedly falls apart. The various ways in which the cauldron is used and misused in the myth illustrates the uses and misuses of Eros. Eros is the archetypal principle of relatedness, "a blind force, fecund and cruel, creating, cherishing and destroying." As the force of affiliation and relatedness, Eros is very close to our cultural definition of the feminine. Jung spoke of Eros as woman's "essential nature."[4] Eros is not, in Jung's thinking, the equivalent of love. It is the primal urge to get involved, to take part and be a part of emotional life, to connect to feelings and people, to get into the middle of human intercourse. Eros does not have exclusively positive effects on people; for example, Lauren's connection to her lover was strong, but not positive. People may also be strongly connected through hate.

Logos, strongly associated with masculinity, complements Eros. Logos is the archetypal principle of knowledge, rationality, discrimination, and achievement. In Jung's theory, the two archetypal psychological principles, Eros and Logos, are equal. Psychologically, Logos divides, categorizes, and seeks to know, while "it is the function of Eros to unite what Logos has sundered."[5] The ideal, in individuals or in a culture, is a balanced mixture of the two.[6] The ideal equilibrium between Logos and Eros would provide a system of checks and balances. The erotic urge to always connect and preserve connection, no matter what the cost, would be checked by a Logos-driven urge to understand. The logical drive to take everything apart analytically would be counterbalanced by the Eros-driven desire for attachment. Pragmatically, people in relationships would take both thought and feeling into account when assessing the viability of a relationship.

Unfortunately the imbalance between masculine and feminine values which so dominates our world view seeps into Jung's explication of a feminized Eros and masculinized Logos. As a consequence, we find consciousness itself described as if it were properly or inherently dominated by Logos, which amounts to saying that consciousness is masculine. Bianca, a recently promoted administrator with a strikingly feminine appearance, felt this very strongly. "In some way," she said, "it seems that to become more conscious is to become more male." Meanwhile, Eros is experienced as passive, primitive, and unconscious.[7] The influence of Western culture's masculine ego ideal subverts Jung's attempt to present Eros and Logos as equal forces in a complementary relationship. The duality, as it is played out in Western culture, is not a complementarity but a split, analogous to the split between autonomy and intimacy, or between masculine and feminine.

Are these gender assignments inevitable? Are they inherent in sexual difference? If you possess a female flesh envelope, are you essentially an agent of Eros, an embodiment of a certain set of immanent values and characteristics? We came up against this question in previous chapters, when discussing gender differences, and it will continue to dog our steps. Historically, the notion of an inferior essential nature in women (or in members of a particular culture or race) has been used to oppress, constrict, and demean, while the notion of a superior essential nature in men (or in, for example, Aryan men) has been used to empower and exalt. Now attempts are being made to reverse the direction of this process by positing an essential superiority in women. Consequently, the question of whether women possess an "essential nature" is a politically charged question and one which, as I stated previously, I do not believe we can answer definitively. For the purposes of this discussion, I will simply note that, after five thousand years of equating the Feminine with Eros, the female affinity for Eros functions for most women as if it were inherent. A given individual woman may not experience it that way, but the majority appear to.

One of the positive aspects of Eros is its psychological power to rejuvenate. Women often seem to believe that they are able to rejuvenate or save those they love, that they are in fact obligated to do so. This is an expression of the strong association of Eros with the Feminine. The force of this obligation is such that, when women are caught up in the destructive side of Eros, when they experience painful disconnections in relationships, they see these interpersonal difficulties as a solely personal failing. Bianca felt tremendous guilt every time she considered a career option that was not comfortable for her partner. Her sense of obligation to the man she was with seemed to have to do with a fear of leaving him high and dry, without the necessary enlivening sustenance of her total attention. The positive power of Eros was experienced by her as a personal obligation. The negative, disruptive aspect of Eros was experienced as a personal flaw. As Bianca put it, "I felt that there was really something wrong with me, that the problems in my relationships proved that."

The shadow side of Eros, vividly symbolized by the witch and her cauldron, is an inherent part of the quest for intimacy. The powerful erotic urge to connect, to be deeply involved with others is, in its light aspect, rejuvenating. In its shadow aspect, Eros can consume and destroy. In

Medea's story, the two aspects of Eros function together in the cauldron—dismembering and regenerating in a continuous flow. In the contemporary Western world, these functions are split and perceived as mutually exclusive. Intimacy and love are idealized, spoken of, and pictured as if they always have positive effects on the individual. When relationships produce negative effects, when the shadow aspect of Eros inevitably and necessarily emerges, it is not seen as a natural part of intimate life.

A fantasy pervades our stories, ideas, and images about intimate connections. The fantasy is that intimacy can be perfect, can be made shadow-free, that the shadow side of Eros can be suppressed. When Cora describes the "ideal vision" she pursued in her relationship, she is describing a version of this fantasy. The fantasy splits the power of Eros into positive and negative sides with each side embodied in certain female images. The positive side of the split is represented by the image of the devoted wife and mother, the negative side by the image of the destructive witch. If a woman is a good, devoted partner she can, in this fantasy, make Eros entirely positive and rejuvenating. If she cannot make her relationships exclusively rejuvenating, if she cannot exclude the shadow of Eros from her intimate relationships, she is seen as destructive. When Cora's ideal vision failed to materialize, her first impulse was to scrutinize herself for the cause of the failure. Women seem to deal with this split between the good, generative woman and the bad, destructive witch by trying to carry and fix the shadow side personally, by identifying certain parts of themselves as dangerous to intimacy and trying to suppress those parts of the self, thus deepening a divide within the self. This divide within the self is connected to a split in our perception of nature and the world.

THIS WORLD IS NOT MY HOME

Growing up in the Bible Belt, I heard a lot of revival preaching. "This world is not my home," one preacher always cried. It was a refrain for him, a dramatic punctuation for his sermon that was always answered with a chorus of "Amens" from the congregation. Once I was grown and gone, I found out that it was a phrase with a history in fundamentalist Christian theology.[8] As with many fundamentalist catch phrases, "this world is not my home" distills a basic element of the Christian world view into an emotional, dramatic exhortation.

In the fifth century, Saint Augustine articulated that world view in a way that came to dominate Church dogma. According to Augustine, nature itself was ruined by Adam's and, more clearly, Eve's original sin. The natural world, the inevitable sufferings and pleasures of living in the world, are all tainted by sin, "made miserable" by it.[9] The only hope of escaping this diseased and intrinsically corrupt world is to aspire to heaven, the real home of our true, spiritual, disembodied selves. To reach this goal, we must transcend being human, separate ourselves from nature, and achieve redemption by denying the body and, ultimately, by dying. In short, "This world is not my home."[10]

Why am I bringing this up? A fifth-century Catholic theologian and a twentieth-century preacher from an obscure Protestant sect have the same world view. So what? It is important because this is the dominant Western world view, pervasive and consistent. Augustine's view was adopted as the state religion of the late Roman Empire; for centuries the Church enforced this dogma through such measures as the Crusades and the Inquisition, in which deviant beliefs were punished with death. From village to university, deviation from this dogma was deemed heresy, punishable by torture and death. As a result, a central idea of Augustine's dogma—the idea that nature and human nature must be controlled and transcended—permeates Western culture and is absorbed by everyone raised in it.[11] It is by no means necessary to be a Christian to hold this world view. In April 1997, members of the Heaven's Gate cult committed suicide in order to transcend the earth, evolve beyond their bodies, and achieve their "true home" in outer space.[12] This world was not their home.

But even though this world is not to be our home, it is a woman's job to *make* a home here. The mundane details of food, cleaning, organizing, and tending to bodily needs, all of the everyday messes, typically and almost exclusively fall to women. The feminine attends to emotional mess as well. Expressing emotions and comforting others who are having strong feelings is womanly, in our view. "Women's work is never done" because all of these things are part of the everyday, natural round. They are never "done" because the body and the emotions run on the cyclical mode, the mode of the natural world, of which the body and the emotions are an inextricable part. The feminine, and individual women as embodiments of the feminine, is nature, is the mundane, and, consequently, the feminine must be transcended even by women themselves.[13]

Here we encounter, on a deeper level, the same paradox or double bind that was portrayed in Broverman's research.

A woman who is healthy as a person, who pursues the dominant values of our culture by rising above the mundane, is sick as a woman because she is not tending to the mundane. One who is healthy as a woman, who attends to all of the messy, cyclical duties assigned to the feminine, is sick as a person because she will never rise above nature.[14] When Lauren describes her ongoing ruminations about her obligations to her partners—should I be in the library [doing research], should I be at home?—she is caught in this double bind. An admirable person pursues excellence in the library, an admirable woman goes home and looks after family. Women as individuals look after the ignored, denigrated, but necessary, shadow side of everyday life. The Feminine, as a category, holds the ignored, denigrated, but necessary shadow side of human experience. In Jungian terms, women become personal and cultural shadow carriers.[15]

Once again we find women as individuals and the feminine as a category associated with the problematic side of a dualistic split, associated with the supposedly inferior side of the split, as both shadow carrier and redeemer. Women and the feminine are all obstacles to the Western project of the transcendence of nature. At the same time women and the feminine are a refuge from the alienation, loss of meaning, and disenchantment, which transcending nature produces. This is a double bind for women, a situation in which they can neither feel good about being associated with nature nor can they feel good about trying to transcend nature. This fundamental contradiction underlies the quest for intimacy, in that it has a profound effect on a woman's efforts to make a home in the world for herself and her loved ones, and a particular effect on how she feels about those efforts.

The paradoxical view of women as simultaneous threat and refuge is mirrored in women's views of themselves. Even if a woman consciously believes that this world is not her home, that the domestic, everyday world must be overcome if she is to have a meaningful life, she may well live her everyday life in contradiction to that conscious belief. She is likely to order her own personal priorities in a way that endorses the profound meaning of everyday life, lived at home. This contradiction frequently remains unconscious, and produces a double bind for the individual woman, a bind in which neither goal, to transcend the world or to make a home in it, can be pursued without producing guilt concerning the opposite goal. How can she transcend the world while being responsible for making a cozy refuge *in* the world, for herself and her loved ones? No amount of hard work and sincere effort will resolve such a double bind, particularly when it remains unconscious.

Unresolved double binds tend to produce psychological symptoms. One of the more important symptoms caused by the double bind that women experience is that many, many women hate their own bodies.[16] Women tend to be obsessed with their bodies, obsessed with the need to overcome, or we could say transcend, the flaws they see in their bodies. Although this obsession seems vain, it rarely provides narcissistic pleasure since the obsession is usually negative. If I know a woman well enough to know her image of her body, then I will know her list of her body's supposed physical defects. This list is almost always in the background of her mind and has been since adolescence, if not before. Much has been written attributing this kind of obsession to the influence of commercial images of the ideal woman.[17] I think, however, that underlying both the commercial images and the individual obsessions, is a fundamental, unresolvable conflict: a woman simply can't be both in the world and out of it at the same time.

In popular imagery, the female body is, when perfect, symbolic of all that is extraordinary in life. Throughout the history of Western art, the female body has been used to personify beauty, truth, and redemption. Modern advertising's use of the female image to make consumer goods desirable is a degraded form of this ancient iconographic tradition. When the female body is imperfect, according to the changeable standards of the given moment, it is symbolic of an intrinsically corrupt natural world, representing the terrors of decay and loss. Women try to live with being the targets of these powerful, contradictory projections by trying to perfect their bodies, or at least by feeling really bad if they can't make their bodies perfect. Cora found that, in one of her most difficult relationships, her image of her body became very negative, as though her body's supposed imperfections were the source of the relationship's difficulties. The piercing pain she felt at that time is still audible in her voice, years later.

Woman's attempt to do the impossible with her own body—that is, to make it perfect and keep it perfect—is an expression and a symptom of the double bind she is in. Her paradoxical effort to make a home in the world while simultaneously rising above the world begins with her body. She can be at home in her body only if it is perfect—perfectly in control, slim, smooth, polished, well dressed, ad infinitum. In short, she can love herself only if she has risen above the very nature of having a body, of being incarnate, imperfect, and vulnerable. Her effort to feel at peace with the female body is an effort to transcend that body's very nature—its ampleness, its curves, its reproductive messiness, its vulnerability. There are two ways in which this effort is impossible. First, if a body could be made physically perfect, the fact that perfection has been bought at the expense of the body's real nature means that this perfection is a form of alienation from the self, and such an alienation can never produce a feeling of peace. Second, a body is never, by its nature, perfect. It changes from moment to moment; it is, by nature, cyclical. Consequently, its flaws must be, at the very least, a source of shame, at the worst a source of self-destructive behavior, such as anorexia and bulimia.

The tormented double bind that women face with their bodies is the most obvious manifestation of the paradoxical forces that govern a woman's search for meaningful relationships. If a woman can accept her body in its true nature, and if she can choose a partner who is capable of doing the same, she may experience real intimacy. But, for the most part women believe that it is only by rejecting their bodies' real nature and striving for an artificial perfection that they can be worthy of intimacy. The pursuit of worthiness through the transcendence of nature begins for a woman with her own natural, physical self. In so far as she is committed to that pursuit, she is cut off from nature's ability to renew and regenerate life in herself and others. She is divided within herself, just as her culture is divided.

A seeker in the quest for intimacy encounters a number of splits or divisions. We have already delineated the deep division between male and female attitudes, aptitudes, and priorities in regard to relationships. This fundamental split reflects a larger opposition in culture, the opposition between a masculinized ego ideal that upholds Logos and a feminized collective shadow that holds Eros. The principle of Eros is then further split into a positive, nurturing, generative side and a negative, devouring, dismembering side. Women embody these splits, both in culture's collective imagery and in their own self-images. Women carry the unacknowledged, unsolved shadow aspects of these splits, both for the collective (where the shadow carrier is an image and idea, "The Feminine") and for the individuals with whom they are intimate, particularly if those individuals are men. All of this contributes greatly to women's sense of being distant from the values of the external world. The divide between a woman's inner world and our culture's outer world is often severe. As we have discussed, the search for meaningful relationships is in part an attempt to bridge this divide. These attempts begin in childhood.

In Western culture, childhood is typically an enclosed female world; ideally, a refuge of togetherness. At some point, certainly by school age or perhaps sooner, the child must begin to negotiate a connection to the world outside, a world with a strong masculine cast. Children try to do this through a process called "identificatory love." This is a natural process in which an adult who seems connected to, and competent in, the outside world is the object of identification for the child. Through trying to be like and feel like this adult, through identifying with him, the child is trying to take in the traits and capacities necessary to make a place for herself in the outside world. How to work, achieve, compete, persevere, protect oneself, in short all of the traits that one needs to leave home, must be learned while the child is still safely at home. In most families and in the culture at large, the adult most identified with the outside world is probably a man, the child's father. Boys are encouraged to pursue identification with their fathers or father figures completely, leaving the female world of childhood as far behind as possible. Girls are in a different position, as we have already discussed in chapter three. How are they to identify with the ability to act in the outside world, to develop the traits in themselves that they find in their fathers, while also preserving a female identity, springing from the powerful connection and identification with the mother that usually constitutes their core sense of self?

This question is not simply an issue of childhood development but remains active in adulthood. Women continue to look for relationships that will help them figure out how to express themselves in the world at large, and they frequently fall in love with people who in some way might give them the help with this that their own fathers did not. As psychoanalyst Jessica Benjamin puts it, "Identification remains part of love relationships throughout life."[18] Women unconsciously tend to identify with someone who has what they lack. They do this through intimate relationships, by trying to have or by having a particular kind of connection with a particular kind of man, to bring the needed traits, abilities, and attitudes into their lives. The process of identifying with and falling in love with a man who seems to have the relationship to the world that you, however unconsciously, feel that you need, is part of projecting the animus onto one's partner. The needed traits are not developed within the self but instead are pursued through trying to unite with a partner who has those qualities. Cora, for example, tended to choose partners who embodied the self-confidence that she was struggling to develop in herself. In the short term this made her feel better, as though she might be able to draw on her partner's confidence. In the long term, such a projection, if not resolved, becomes an impediment to individuation.

Medea pursues this union on a transpersonal scale. In one way, her story can be seen as a metaphor for the relationship between Eros and Logos in a patriarchal culture. Medea's magic is, perhaps, a manifestation of the Eros power of the old goddesses. Robert Graves, in his analysis of Greek myth, sees Medea as an aspect of the old Great Goddess of the prehistoric Mediterranean.[19] Her Cauldron of Regeneration, dragon enchantments, and skill in transformations are important remnants of Medea's origin as a goddess of death and regeneration, probably associated with the moon in both its light and dark aspects. Her connection to Jason and her foray into his patriarchal world narrates an attempt to connect the archaic matriarchal culture of the goddess worshipers to the politically dominant culture of the patriarchal Greeks.

Medea is connected to a lost realm in which the passion of nature, the light and shadow of Eros in everyday life was embodied in the goddess. The goddess made a home for her worshipers in the world. Medea's quest takes her from that home into the patriarchal realm of Jason's Greece. Her quest attempts to bring the multilayered, interrelated world view of the goddess into relationship to an outside world, dominated by the very masculine values of classical Greek culture. In this endeavor, Jason functions as the animus-mediator who will facilitate the connection between Medea's inner world and the outer world. This portrays, in archetypal terms, an aspect of the quest for intimacy that we have already discussed in individual terms—that is, the attempt to connect, through intimate partnership, a feminine inner world of malleable, interpenetrated boundaries with a crisply defined and categorized masculine outer world.

There are a number of ancient Greek stories about relationships between women of goddess cultures and patriarchal Greeks, including the story of Medea's aunt, Circe, the island witch. Throughout Greek myth, gods and heroes encounter women, often rather strange women, whom they marry, kidnap, rape, or rescue. These are sometimes called "conquered female" stories, and, interestingly, the plots often resemble contemporary romance novels. These episodes have been understood in a number of ways, most commonly as portrayals of historical conquests, in which the Greek god or hero overcomes a female figure who symbolizes a people who have, in fact, been conquered by the Greeks.[20] In this way, through the story, a colonized "barbarian" land becomes a part of Greek mythic cosmology.[21] Some mythographers think that the colonized people and land are represented by a woman in these stories because both barbarians and women are "other" in Greek patriarchal culture, both are categories of people who need to be controlled and civilized by Greek masculine order. Others think that the appropriated female symbolizes a specifically matriarchal culture whose conquest is symbolically portrayed in myth, that the female figure represents a Great Goddess from a preexisting matriarchal society, whose power and prerogatives are being usurped by a patriarchal agent in the myth, a hero representing Greek culture.[22]

Circe's story is both like and unlike these conquest stories.[23] Although the hero, Odysseus (another name for Ulysses), becomes her lover, her island is not conquered and she is not carried away on his ship. Neither she nor her land is colonized, so her story differs from the usual. Her special ways with animals and potions give her a witchy aura. Her sacred grove and transformative powers indicate that she is a moon goddess, showing light and dark aspects, as befits a relative of Medea's.

Circe's island was a mystical grove in which men might be turned into swine. Circe was, as Odysseus and his crew discovered when their wanderings took them to the island, skilled with drugs and transformations. When they trespassed on her precincts, she turned the crew into pigs. Her power was both baleful and fertile (she bore Odysseus three sons before allowing him to sail on). In the various versions of Odysseus's tale, she is sometimes called a goddess, sometimes a witch. Circe in some ways functions as an initiatrix for the patriarchal hero Odysseus, initiating him into a liminal, mysterious way of life in which strict categories and masculine values are superseded.[24] But when Odysseus moves on, there is no sign that he takes any of her world view with him.

On her island, Circe lives split off from the patriarchal new world order of the Greeks. This may represent the historical persistence of isolated pockets of matriarchal culture, scattered through the territory dominated by the

Greeks. It also portrays the way in which the mystery of life and nature embodied in the figure of the multifaceted goddess was split off, marginalized in consciousness—perhaps forgotten and, if encountered by chance, left unconnected to the rest of life. Bianca used a turn of phrase during my conversation with her that reminded me of Circe. She was speaking of her sense of having found an inner, spiritual base for her life, one that seemed solid, fitting, and sure. She ended by saying "Here I am on dry land; I made it. Will a man come to my shore?" Circe stays on her island, unchanged by her encounter with patriarchy but detached from the mainstream of conscious life. She, and the way of life she embodies, become irrelevant to the hero's journey as it continues, in much the same way that a man's mother is supposed, according to our ego ideal, to become irrelevant to his adult life. A lovely memory, perhaps, but irrelevant to the most important part of adult life.

Medea, who shares so many of Circe's divine attributes—the sacred grove in which the fleece hangs, transformative powers, efficacy with herbs and drugs—also falls in love with a patriarchal hero. But she does not stay, unchanged, in her sacred grove as Circe does. Neither is she completely consumed by the new world order, as are the women in the "conquered female" stories. Instead Medea attempts to connect the insular (because it is besieged) female world of the goddess to the outer world of the Greek heroes. Medea's many acts of magic are in service to Jason's purposes but could also be seen as an attempt to bring the realities of an Eros-based world view into relationship to the Logos-driven mainstream. The cauldron in particular is a symbol of the power of Eros, taken out of the sacred grove and used in the patriarchal world.[25]

I think that this is part of Medea's quest, to make a functional partnership between matriarchy and patriarchy. She neither stays split off from the dominant world order, like Circe, nor is she destroyed by it. She leaves her isolation, goes into the center of the patriarchal world and interacts with it, first through her relationship to Jason, later with others. Hers is the female quest, as we have already described it—bringing the inner world into relationship to the outer world, manifesting this layered internal experience in external life through a primary partnership and the creation of a new family—writ large in cultural terms. In those terms, successful intimacy with Jason symbolizes the interweaving of Eros and Logos. The separate worlds of Medea and Jason still exist, and not just as personal experiences. The overt, patriarchal, Logos-run dominant culture and the insular, feminine, Eros-driven muted culture are still split. Every heterosexual relationship is an attempt to bridge that split, so that the power of Eros, in the form of feminine values, can be brought to bear on a masculinist, Logos-run world through the medium of relationship.[26]

This attempt to bridge the divide through relationship is generally unconscious. Cora, however, was consciously concerned with finding a place in the world for her spiritual beliefs, and she thought, at one time, that she had found the perfect partner for that project. "The idealization [of my new partner] was activated again. The partnership had more to it than the previous one and I idealized him more. This person was outwardly bolstering to my self-esteem, but later I realized he had a deep, unspoken contempt for me, for women. That relationship nearly killed me. I didn't get it, how perilous it was, until my body was falling apart. I got into a death struggle, I was fighting for my life. Despite what I had learned in previous relationships about the need for respect, I repeated the pattern of idealizing a man who was condescending. I repeated it at a much subtler turn of the spiral. I kept thinking it would come true this time, that it would be good for me, emotionally and spiritually."

In Cora's story I hear again the questing passion, the activation of an archetypal pattern in which one perseveres, overcomes all obstacles, and finally, at whatever cost, achieves the quest. It may nearly kill you, but in the end you will find spiritual gold, salvation, redemption. Your inner image of truth and reality is manifested in the world through the medium of a meaningful relationship. In Guggenbühl-Craig's terms, Cora puts well-being aside in order "to authentically pursue life's meaning and the development of the soul in a partnership."[27] She was pursuing salvation and individuation through this relationship, searching for authenticity and meaning, even though, in this case, the quest did not result in a healthy, intimate relationship.

THE MEANINGFUL RELATIONSHIP AS A SPIRITUAL ISSUE

In addition to carrying the unsolved interpersonal and emotional problems of patriarchal culture, women may be carrying an unsolved problem on the spiritual level—the problem of alienation from nature and Eros, the difficulty of reestablishing a sense of "at-homeness" for self and family in a disenchanted world, a world in which alienation from nature and the trivialization of everyday life has made meaning hard to find. This, in my opinion, is a deeper, more than personal purpose of the search for meaningful relationships, even if it is an unarticulated and, for most women, an unconscious purpose.

I am proposing that the quest for intimacy is on some level a transpersonal or spiritual quest. I realize that in doing so I may sound radical. Our culture is so alienated from Eros-oriented spiritual meaning that it is hard to even find appropriate language to express the spiritual nature of the quest for intimacy. Jean Baker Miller has articulated the difficulty of articulating such unconventional experiences especially well: "The ways we find to conceptualize our experience are in large measure given to us by the culture in which we learn how to think and how to feel or even learn what thinking and feeling are. But people are also continually straining against the boundaries of their culture— against the limiting categories given by that culture—and seeking the means to understand and to express the many experiences for which it does not suffice. This is true for all people. For women today it is a preeminent factor. As we have seen there are fundamental reasons why women do not easily find the means at hand to conceptualize and express their experiences. But they are struggling to develop those means."[28] An ideal vision of a relationship, like Cora's, is simultaneously a problematic fantasy and an effort to imagine something beyond the limiting categories bequeathed to her by her culture.

It isn't easy to discuss the possible spiritual implications and meaning of women's efforts to forge an intimate partnership that will act as a refuge, a home in a material world that is, according to their culture's values, inherently without spiritual meaning. Some women continue, consciously or unconsciously, with or without support, directly or indirectly, to struggle with the effort to connect feminine values to a masculine world, to mediate the harshness of a disenchanted world. As women struggle, suffer, and cope with this impossible task (impossible for an individual to resolve unilaterally, in any case), they are surely injured by it. But are they also enriched by this kind of struggle?

Peter Gomes, the chaplain of Harvard University, thinks that the struggles of those on the margins of society can give them spiritual insight. To explain this, Gomes borrows the concept of "thin places" from Celtic mythology. For the ancient Celts, thin places were gateways between the visible and invisible worlds, between ordinary reality and spiritual reality (or, psychologically, between personal experience and transpersonal experience). At certain points, the boundaries between these seemingly divided realms become permeable, or "thin," allowing connection between separated worlds. For Gomes, human experiences of mystery and suffering can be "thin places," functioning as gateways to spiritual resources. Since societal outcasts experience more suffering and possibly more mystery than those who fit the dominant mold, he speculates that "outcasts may well be the custodians of those thin places; they may in fact be the watchers at the frontier between what is and what is to be." Because of this, "the place for creative hope that arises out of suffering is most likely to be found among blacks, women, and homosexuals."[29]

Is this mere idealization of the victim role? Or by using Gomes's concepts to reflect on the spiritual meaning of women's quest for intimacy, am I touting the moral superiority of women? I don't think that we have to resort to a notion of essential goodness in order to find Gomes's ideas useful. He is saying that the view from the edge of the mainstream inevitably provides perspectives which are not available to those being pulled along at the center of the current. A secretary knows very different things about a corporation than a vice president does, and some of those things will be very important. Many of them will be from the shadow side of the collective experience. For Jung, the shadow is the threshold of the unconscious and its resources. This perspective on the shadow side of experience could give the outcast increased, more vivid contact with the wellspring of unconscious human potentials that are unacknowledged by the mainstream world view. These resources are personal and transpersonal in nature.

The transpersonal, spiritual dimensions of the quest for intimacy may give women added strength, accounting for some of their tremendous resilience and determination in relationships. But the fact that the quest has a deeper meaning also "pumps up" the feeling level, so that the ups and downs of relationships, the normal failures of intimacy take on life and death meaning. Some women are prompted to give larger than life, mythic responses to these ups and downs, especially if the spiritual aspect of the quest is active, though unconscious. Inflated responses may range from martyrdom to revenge. Medea's use of the Cauldron of Regeneration for purposes of revenge is a foreshadowing of more spectacular reactions to come. The transformative bases of Medea's magic, the power of Eros evident in the cauldron, is misappropriated in the Pelias episode. A more spectacular and problematic misuse of relationship magic, which we will look at in the next chapter, will end Medea's intimacy with Jason.

CHAPTER FIVE

The Shadow of the Search for Intimacy

MEDEA AND JASON settled in Corinth, where Medea was the only surviving descendent of the Corinthian royal house. The Corinthians accepted them as king and queen. They ruled there for ten years, apparently happy, and had many children. Then Jason decided he wanted to marry a young and beautiful Theban princess, the daughter of the powerful tyrant Creon. His wife reminded him of his oath of loyalty, but he remained obstinate, claiming that a forced oath is invalid. Medea pointed out that he owed the Corinthian throne to her, but Jason claimed that the Corinthians would support him because they liked him better than they liked her.

Medea, feigning acceptance, sent the princess a wedding gift, a robe which, when put on, burst into unquenchable flames. The princess ran in desperation through the wedding party, spreading the flames so that the palace, the wedding guests, and Creon were all consumed with the bride. Only Jason escaped the fire, by jumping from an upstairs window. Medea fled Corinth. Some say that to complete her revenge, she killed her children before she ran. Others say that she told them to take refuge in Hera's temple, where the enraged Corinthians slaughtered them.

Medea has made an extraordinary commitment to Jason, giving up her former life and attachments in order to forge a partnership with him. Although she extracts an oath of loyalty from him, in the end he does not feel bound by the oath. This is not surprising to anyone, except perhaps Medea. Jason's entire career has been based on trickiness and secret dealings, many of which Medea has helped him to carry out. Yet when he does with her what he has done with everyone else, i.e., when he duplicitously pursues his own ambition at her expense, she is enraged, shocked, and extraordinarily vengeful. Apparently she expected Jason to behave in a special way with her, in a way very different from his behavior in other relationships.

Like Medea, the wife who has sacrificed for her family and for her husband's career only to be abandoned is a figure that evokes strong reactions. These reactions reflect the split we have already found in our views of women's devotion to relationships. Many people believe that such a woman has earned the continuity of the relationship through her work and sacrifice. Others feel that this constitutes an expectation of payment for devotion, unpleasantly echoing the classic reproach of the grasping mother: "After all I've done for you." Both of these reactions focus on the external appearance of justice or lack of it. Is a woman in this position a victim or a parasite? Is she entitled to her resentment, or should she just get a life?

The discarded, resentful woman has become a cliché in popular culture. "I gave up the best years of my life for you" is her battle cry. However trite this sounds, it may be an accurate statement in relationships that have been maintained more by the woman's dedication to intimacy than by genuine understanding between the partners. Working the magic of maintaining partnerships that are not based on real compatibility requires a woman to give up a lot of herself. She offers up her self-interest for the sake of the relationship, and, consciously or unconsciously, she expects to be rewarded for this sacrifice, to be made special by it.

Her partner may not respond to this stance with appreciation. Instead, continual sacrifice may breed an expectation in her partner of more of the same, an expectation of further, perhaps complete sacrifice of her self-interest. It seems in such situations that the woman has not asked herself, "What sort of person would be comfortable with the kind of sacrifice I'm making? If my partner is happy with this what does it say about his character and likely behavior?" The woman seems to imagine that her partner will act against reasonable expectations given his previous behavior, and that something special and out of character will happen, perhaps for both partners. This wish or hope is perhaps an expression of the effort to reenchant life, to make the everyday special. When these expectations are disappointed, various kinds of overt and covert revenge may be pursued, often involving children.

Medea's revenge is what most people remember about her story. She is the ultimate bad wife and mother, violator of the most sacred code of spousal loyalty, womanly gentleness, and maternal love; she is a Betty Broderick acquitted, a Susan Smith who escapes punishment. But Medea's revenge has a psychologically meaningful prelude: the scene is set for the revenge in a way that tells us something important about the search for meaningful relationships. Medea has, to all appearances, achieved her quest—she has intimacy, of a sort, with Jason. She has established a new family with him. But the foundation of her achievement is seriously flawed, and these flaws play themselves out in a way that, despite its bloody melodrama, is familiar to us. The foundational problems of the marriage emerge over time in a way that we still see in contemporary life.

For instance, in the fall of 1996, the actress Claire Bloom published a memoir about her marriage to the novelist Philip Roth. She described herself as a victim of his domination and misogyny. The book provoked commentary rather similar to the commentary on Hannah Arendt I discussed in chapter two. Patricia Bosworth in the *New York Times Book Review* states that Bloom acts "as if she believed her strength as a woman was best expressed by giving herself away. It is difficult to accept such behavior, especially when you consider Ms. Bloom's achievements."[1] The clear implication, as with Arendt, is that we just can't imagine why a smart, talented, accomplished woman with a life of her own, with achievements, would sacrifice to maintain a relationship with a problematic partner. In fact, the belief Bosworth accuses Bloom of holding, that womanly strength is based on the ability to give oneself away, is at the heart of relationship magic. It is both an implicit and explicit aspect of the female quest for intimacy. As such, self-sacrifice is not contradicted by Bloom's achievements; it is rather a type of achievement itself.

Another reviewer asks, "But where in any of this is Bloom's own, highly formidable will, . . . that steely instrument" that propelled her to success?[2] Her will was bent to the task of establishing and maintaining intimacy. Having achieved the object of her quest, intimacy with Roth, she set about preserving it. Perhaps it is obvious now that she was attempting to be intimate with what was, for her, an impossible partner. When this unworkable marriage crumbled, Bloom exacted a Medea-like revenge, dismembering Roth in the public forum of her book. Both her dedication to the relationship and the revenge that followed its demise are an expression of her formidable will, not a denial of it. This type of assertion of will is one that we see women make in many failed partnerships; first they will themselves to achieve an impossible union and then to exact revenge after its failure. Why do women use their strength in this way?

THE IMPOSSIBLE PARTNER

When we think about the impossible partner, the image of Bluebeard returns. What about all of the women—apparently there have been quite a few who fell for his approach—who fail to notice his blue beard, who fail to take in the implications of his mysteriously missing previous wives? Why do they imagine that Bluebeard is a possible partner? What special thing do women think is going to happen that will change such a man in an intimate partnership? Do they see themselves as having a special power, a power that will make the impossible partner possible? I don't think so. I think that something more complex is going on. When a woman has made a strong attachment to a man, she begins to experience his behavior as meaningful about *herself,* rather than meaningful about him. Frequently, when a female psychotherapy client describes something her spouse has done that she dislikes, she will immediately go on to describe all of the things she could or should have done to change his action. These range from retrospective speculations—"I should have said this, shouldn't have said that"—to more vague and general assertions that amount to, "If I were more lovable he wouldn't behave this way." The notion that the other person might have their own, separate, reasons for their behavior or that the behavior is, at least, the product of some mutual interaction, is one that has not even been considered. These women see themselves as the root cause of all problems.

Although there is certainly a touch of grandiosity in this skewed perspective on interpersonal responsibility, it is more significant as an illustration of a woman's malleable interpersonal boundaries and of her sense of one-sided responsibility for intimacy. It reflects the unilateral obligation women feel for creating a meaningful, smoothly running relationship, for reenchanting life with intimacy. Typically both men and women imagine, without really articulating the fantasy, that the woman in a partnership will exert "relationship magic," or what Betty Friedan called the "feminine mystique,"[3] causing the relationship to work smoothly. If it doesn't work smoothly, blame is, consciously or unconsciously, assigned to the woman. She is shirking her duty as the resident relationship magician.

The belief that women are responsible for the behavior of their partners is widespread. In a startling example, Nafis Sadik, a United Nations officer, experienced a very direct version of this notion in a private audience with Pope John Paul II. In discussing the circumstances of poor and abandoned women with children in third world countries, the Pontiff said to her, "Don't you think that the irresponsible behavior of men is caused by women?"[4] This is a shockingly obvious instance of victim blaming, but I am struck by how passionately this is believed by women themselves. Their unilateral responsibility for intimacy frequently translates into a feeling of responsibility for their partner's actions within the relationship. Thus difficulties with the impossible partner are experienced as a problem within the self, not as an interpersonal dilemma. If the problem is felt to be *within the self*, then work on the self will make the impossible partner possible.

The impossibility of certain partners is further obscured by the complexity of the quest for intimacy. It seems that more is being sought by women than simple togetherness with another human being, that the quest carries both psychological and collective cultural baggage. Psychologically, women may be seeking a relationship that will allow them to realize their inner world in an authentic way, a way denied to them by the culture at large. Collectively, women may be seeking to reenchant life for themselves and their loved ones, to make a meaningful home in a disenchanted world, to create a partnership that embodies feminine values in a culture that denies them. The position of women and of the feminine in the Western world encourages them to carry this baggage, consciously or unconsciously, willingly or unwillingly, but always without social recognition of any significant kind. Women learn to pursue their quest and carry this baggage, using "relationship magic," which is composed of skills, priorities, and values that are generally unseen and unacknowledged. Because this baggage being carried by the quest for intimacy is not acknowledged, the difficulty of managing it is ignored. Because the skills and values women use to perform relationship magic are unrecognized, the price women pay in order to exercise them is not acknowledged. The impossible partner may not, in this context, seem much more impossible than any other part of the quest.

Women are praised in public for devotion and self-sacrifice in relationships. If you think about any campaign speech you've heard in which a male candidate refers to his wife, or if you take a look at the dedications of books by male authors, you will find many instances of fulsome praise for the saintly relational woman. Yet, if this is so, why am I saying that women's work on togetherness is not recognized? True recognition, the kind that can be felt by a person as acknowledgment, springs from a realistic perception of what is being done by that person, its effect and its cost. For women, and for the feminine as a category, there is mystique instead of acknowledgment, blanket idealization rather than the careful observation of individual effort that leads to recognition.

The tendency to idealize and generalize women's devotion to relationship is evident not only in American culture at large but also in a range of psychological theories. Traditional Jungian theory identifies women with Eros explicitly and portrays the role of women in relationships in nearly magical terms.[5] The feminist Relational School does something similar, using different terminology.[6] I believe that this encourages individual women to see themselves in less than individual terms, to assess their partners and their relationships in the light of a generalized image of womanly devotion, rather than the light cast by the specific reality in front of them. The partner is not seen clearly and so cannot be recognized as an individual with particular capacities and incapacities. Instead he is seen as someone who can be changed by love into a suitable partner. Lauren's partner can, from outside the relationship, clearly be seen as a person who is not suited to be the partner of a woman who knows her own mind. His wish that his partner agree completely with his perceptions meant that Lauren could not find a workable way of living with him. However, Lauren was unable to see this clearly, in part because of the factors described above.

Lack of recognition of one's partner tends to go hand-in-hand with an obtuseness about one's self. The most basic questions of compatibility—who am I? who do I want to become? who is my partner? who does my partner want to become? do our beliefs and desires fit together in any workable way?—are not asked. Women often ignore the way in which a realistic assessment of the partner is necessary to the development of good relationships. They perceive such clear-eyed assessments as being opposed to real love, destructive to the magic of Eros. How can a woman assess her partner if she is supposed to embody that magic.[7]

When Cora imagined that she could make her vision of the ideal relationship come true despite her partner's behavior, she was not realistically or clearly assessing herself, her partner, or their relationship. She ignored his real personality, or, as she put it, "I probably bypassed his problems." Even when it became clear that Cora and her partner were incompatible, she felt driven to maintain the relationship. "I felt I had to keep trying. I have since discovered that that part of myself has a destructive side. The pain and suffering I felt was not an issue to that part of myself." The pain and suffering were communications from her body and her emotions, telling her that something was terribly wrong with the relationship. But Cora took them as a sign that something was wrong with *her*. She thought that if she could fix whatever that was, she could fix the relationship. She ignored her real self, as it was expressed in her physical and emotional feelings, in order to manifest an idealized self. Likewise, she ignored her partner's real personality in an attempt to fabricate an idealized relationship.

TRYING TO BE SPECIAL BY BEING INAUTHENTIC

What about Medea's real self? Scholars have noted that, in many versions of Medea's story, she is described very differently after she marries Jason than in the episodes preceding marriage. Particularly in Euripides' famous play *Medea* the married Medea is spoken of, by herself, her husband, and others, as if she is an average woman. How could they forget who she was, who she is? How could she forget? Why is Jason, and everyone else, surprised when the woman who enchanted a dragon, murdered her own half-brother, and commanded the Cauldron of Regeneration turns out to be difficult to discard? It looks like Medea has given up a lot of herself in her pursuit of intimacy with Jason. Apparently her authentic self has been subsumed into a generic role— that of the good wife.

It is common these days to speak of the role of the "good wife" as if it is a thing of the past. Certainly its more outrageous forms, such as June Cleaver vacuuming in pearls and heels on "Leave It to Beaver," are rarely seen in contemporary America. But the core traits of the good wife, especially the wifely characteristic of exclusive devotion to the marriage, still exert pressure on women. Even women like Lauren, who have strong independent lives, struggle with the idea of having any priorities other than devotion. As she puts it, "I'm constantly having to convince myself that it's OK to do my own stuff while he's sitting there, to wrap Christmas presents while he's sitting there. I have to keep saying to myself, 'It's OK to do this separate thing.' Of course I know intellectually it's OK to do the separate thing and then to do the together thing, but I have to keep arguing with myself about it. I have to keep consciously assuring myself that 'Yes, this is OK, it really is fine'." What a struggle to choose the self, in the most simple way—I want to wrap Christmas presents!—over the role of devoted wife!

What could Medea be hoping for in playing out a role rather than retaining and expressing her true self? The myth does not tell us but we can speculate. She seems to be forgoing or surrendering the self (the accusation leveled at Claire Bloom) in order to be a suitable relationship partner. Or, it may be more accurate to say that one part of the self becomes highly developed in the service roles of wife and mother. The part of the self that is able to empathize with others very deeply and experience others' needs and personal lives as part of oneself can perhaps be fully realized in the role of wife and mother. The problem lies in the split between this part of the self and the rest of the self. Medea's everyday life seems to have become identified with her relationship with Jason. Meanwhile the parts of the self that are inimical to that identity languish and seem to disappear.

In a recent study, Carol Gilligan found that girls moving into adolescence seem to buy into an image of perfection in relationships. As they became adolescents, Gilligan's subjects began to edit themselves severely, withholding and ignoring any responses within themselves that did not fit their image of a nice person. Consequently, each girl tried to maintain the *appearance* of perfect relationships by learning "not to speak about—and eventually not to know—her thoughts and feelings."[8] Unfortunately, this behavior does not end in adolescence, as we saw in Cora's relationship. As girls become women, ignoring the self and its communications of feeling, preference, reaction, and individual perception, begins to seem necessary to maintain relationships.

What Gilligan says of these adolescent girls, that they "are in danger of losing their ability to distinguish what is true from what is said to be true, what feels loving from what is said to be love, what feels real from what is said to be reality,"[9] plays itself out in the lives of adult women. The general, ideal image of a good, devoted woman in a perfect relationship is pursued at the expense of knowing the self and of truly knowing the other. Intimacy is believed to spring from "perfect" behavior rather than from genuineness, even though the exclusion of the genuine self from relationships renders intimacy unreal and brittle. There is, as Gilligan says, "a paradoxical or dizzying sense of having to give up relationship for the sake of relationships, . . . taking oneself out of relationship in order to protect oneself and have relationships."[10]

Cora described her experience of this split: "The disparity between deeper layers of my self and my outer self-image came out in the relationship. But I kept thinking that if I worked harder [her vision of a partnership] would come true, that it would be good for me, emotionally and spiritually, to work harder." Cora is obviously a thoughtful and perceptive person. How did she come to believe that not being herself might turn out to be good for her? I have framed women's quest for intimacy as an attempt to connect a culturally denied female inner world to a masculinized outer world through an intimate partnership, to create a meaningful relationship that can carry the soul's purpose in everyday life. But here we see women suppressing parts of that inner world, squashing it into conventional forms, in order to maintain intimacy at any cost. The intimacy they are maintaining with its high cost to the self is quite the opposite of the intimacy I believe they have been seeking. What is happening here? Why has the quest for intimacy become so skewed in an unhealthy way?

I think that the lack of reflection in our outer world of woman's inner world creates an immense longing in women for mirroring and recognition. Unconscious bargains are struck by women in which they show only a part of their inner world, the part—usually, but not always, the most service-oriented part—that is most likely be seen and acknowledged. The unconscious nature of this bargain makes it hard to notice that it is a deal that will never pay off. It is unworkable because if a woman's sense of self-worth derives from a deceptive presentation of her self, then she will never have a sense of genuine worth. Every moment of recognition is fatally tainted by the knowledge that it has been gained through subterfuge. A woman who gains acknowledgment in this way feels that "if they only knew how I really feel (or what I really think or what I really want to do, etc.) they wouldn't like me." At the same time, she does not feel confident that the full authentic self, if manifested, can be accepted and valued. Of course, if she has not been careful in choosing her partner, there is an excellent chance that she is right about that.

Women want to feel special, and they look to their relationships as the source of that feeling, as the part of their lives that provides meaning. The only reliable source of specialness, however, is in the development over a lifetime of the authentic self, the process Jung called "individuation." Yet it is also vital that one's true self is recognized by others who are capable of grasping and understanding it, an aspect of individuation that people hope to realize in intimate relationships. As we have noted in previous chapters, women are in a paradoxical situation regarding individuation within relationships. Developing the self and developing intimacy seem opposed to each other, yet a woman is supposed to feel special because of the kind of intimacy she can, or should establish with her life partner. The ability to establish an intimate, domestic sanctuary, to reenchant everyday life for her loved ones is her supposed path to feeling special and worthy. However, the baggage that comes along with the search for meaningful relationships is too much for any individual woman to successfully carry. She cannot feel good about her quest, even when she appears to have achieved it, because of the perceived choice that must be made between self and relationship. She struggles to make herself into the image of someone who can succeed at intimacy, regardless of her true responses to the specific situation in front of her. And this leads to more feelings of failure, because real intimacy can only spring from the real self.

Lauren described her effort to preserve intimacy by ignoring the self in this way: "What kept me there was hoping for change and thinking that nothing is black and white. I would think, 'This is too hard,' but then I would talk myself back into paying attention to the good stuff. Also, I have incredible tolerance for painful situations that I feel I have to put up with." Lauren had reactions and feelings that were trying to let her know that her partner was hurting her. However, she talked herself out of listening to those reactions. This is the road that Gilligan's young subjects have started down, editing and suppressing who they really are, while paradoxically hoping that their relationship partners will, as Lauren has said before, "realize who I really am." Relationships maintained by suppressing the real self are inherently inauthentic. Such relationships lack meaning. As a consequence, they are inherently brittle.

When Jason betrays Medea, he shatters the inauthentic life they have made together. Medea has not achieved the deeper levels of the quest for intimacy. She has not been able to make a bridge between her world and Jason's world, between feminine and masculine approaches to life or make a reliable refuge for her own unique values and meanings. She has not been, and has not been able to be, her true self. She has, instead, been completely subsumed into Jason's patriarchal Greek world. The oath of fidelity has failed to maintain the conditions necessary to a partnered individuation; it has failed to provide the container necessary to the development of the self. The oath was forced and taken for expediency; it was not the end result of any assessment of compatibility, trustworthiness, depth of feeling or character. How many women have forced or insisted on a marriage, seemingly despite the unsuitability of their potential husbands. (This, too, is part of Claire Bloom's story.) In a way, these kinds of relationships are based on people using each other. The woman uses the man to pursue intimacy in an almost impersonal expression of Eros, an expression that discounts his real personality. The man uses the woman's drive for his own purposes, as Jason used Medea.

It would seem, in these situations, that men have more power than women. Certainly my female clients feel this, that the partner who more actively seeks closeness (usually the woman) is in the "one-down" position. Some of this feeling springs from the low status that need has in Western society. Anyone who openly needs something or someone risks contempt, from themselves and from others. Therefore, the partner who appears to need the relationship the most feels humiliated. However, some of these feelings of powerlessness spring from the fact that women make an unconscious attempt to be made "worthy" through a successful relationship. (This fantasy says, in essence, "Make me special, give my life meaning, by being intimate with me.") The woman's attitude toward herself is determined by the success or failure of this attempt. If my partner loves me enough to be intimate, I can feel good about myself. If he doesn't, I can't. She projects—and this is a very strong projection of the role of the animus onto the male—giving him an aura of power. But since both partners in this kind of relationship are, on some level, behaving inauthentically, neither has genuine or useful power. Both have hidden agendas, conscious or unconscious, and are, consequently, at cross-purposes even when the surface of the relationship appears smooth. Bianca and one of her partners conducted a long-distance relationship for a number of years in which, to preserve the relationship, each pretended to accept the other's reasons for being apart. The relationship appeared workable but the pretense of agreement eventually, inevitably, broke down, causing feelings of betrayal on both sides.

Two partners pursuing cross-purposes in an intimate relationship without knowing that their purposes are radically different, will, generally speaking, eventually come to a reckoning. The flaws in the foundation of the partnership will play themselves out, and the woman's relationship magic will prove unequal to the task of maintaining an intimacy that is not based on true mutual understanding. As Lauren put it, "It became an incredible struggle to constantly deal with these situations as the relationship went on—the fun part became less and less, the craziness came out more and more." The craziness is a wake-up call, and sometimes it is quite dramatic. Cora reflected, "What did it take to wake me up? I got into a death struggle, I was fighting for my life." Medea wakes up when Jason decides to leave her. This is probably one of the most common ways in which the hidden contradictions in a relationship play themselves out, in a drama of abandonment and infidelity. The sense of betrayal that follows often leads to covert or overt revenge.

REVENGE AND THE FAILED QUEST FOR INTIMACY

Medea feigns acceptance of Jason's plan to marry the young princess. Her pretense works so well that when she sends the princess a wedding gift, no one is suspicious. The gift is a booby trap, an enchanted robe that bursts into lethal flame. Medea seems to use the fact that everyone has forgotten her sorcery in order to ambush them. The clever ruthlessness of Medea's part in Jason's early adventure has disappeared behind her role of wife and mother. Her swift and merciless retribution takes everyone by surprise, for they had become used to dismissing her, attributing all real power to Jason. The denied part of Medea's identity, her power and her fierceness, are resurrected, literally, with a vengeance.

It is not uncommon for women to lose their sense of self in the role of good wife and mother, and it is not uncommon for them to be perceived as trivial in that role. Although the good wife and mother receives lavish generic praise, individual women who devote themselves to service relationships are often treated with contempt. They are generally perceived as needy, weak, possibly burdensome, and, in many ways, dismissable. Frequently such women go along, martyr-like, with this treatment, perhaps because they feel contempt for themselves, perhaps because they believe it is saintly, in some way, to tolerate contempt. The more thoroughly a woman dedicates herself to classically feminine service roles, the more likely she is to experience the disdain that American culture directs at those who are vulnerable and dependent, who are seen as passive or impotent. Contempt obscures our view of such women just as, in the story, everyone's view of Medea is obscured by their image of her as "only" a wife and mother. This image may even obscure women's views of themselves. Devotion to the service roles of wife and mother can foster a partial identity, not necessarily a false identity but a narrow one. When the relationship that sustains the partial identity is broken, other aspects of the self may emerge, to everyone's surprise.

Medea sets off a conflagration that annihilates the identity she has built in her relationship with Jason. She made a fundamental sacrifice at the beginning of her relationship with Jason. She abandoned her own life path as it was unfolding and bound herself to his. As we have discussed, this kind of sacrifice is made with certain expectations. It initiates a kind of contract in which the personal price exacted by the woman's devotion to maintaining the relationship will be repaid in certain ways. Jason's desire to break his oath of fidelity violates more than the marriage contract. By moving on to another relationship, Jason refuses to continue as Medea's link between the domestic female world and the male outer world. He refuses to continue to carry the power of her animus projection, and he removes the consistent container she needs to bring the disparate parts of herself—Queen, enchantress, mother, mate, and lover—together. There will be no permanent payoff for Medea's devotion, for her willingness to make Jason's path her own.

The payoff for self-sacrifice in relationships is usually dissatisfying, even when the disappointment is less dramatic than Medea's. When a woman devotes herself to maintaining a relationship at all costs, she neglects her own individuation. When she devotes herself to an impossible partner, she takes on an undoable task. When she submerges herself, to the exclusion of developing other parts of the self, in service roles, she courts a future emptiness, an emptiness that descends when her services are no longer needed. Submersion in these roles leads to a detachment from the inner guidance of the self, at least at those points where that inner guidance is counter to the roles. Detachment from the inner guidance of the self gives rise to a sense of emptiness. Returning to the life story of Princess Diana, we can see this scenario unfold. The self-sacrificing roles played by the

Princess of Wales were more dramatic than those enacted by the typical wife and mother, in that she was required to submerge herself in the obligations of royalty as well as family. She was, however, devoted for many years to an impossible partner, an incompatible husband who had long been in love with another woman. Diana's detachment from her own inner guidance, her sense of emptiness, was expressed in dramatic ways—suicidal gestures, incapacitating depression, and bulimia.

As long as the objects of devotion play their parts, the emptiness may not be obvious, to the woman or those who know her. The sacrifice was made for intimacy, and the intimacy, or the appearance or possibility of intimacy, is still there as long as the relationship persists. If the contract has not yet paid off, perhaps it will with more effort or time. This may explain, at least in part, the fact that many women go back, again and again, to unsatisfying relationships. When Hannah Arendt took on Heidegger's problems after World War II, was she hoping that her historical sacrifices would finally pay off, that they would finally have meaning, that she would feel recognized, special?

There are many ways in which a woman may finally realize that such a fantasy contract will never pay off. Her partner may lose all interest in her, her children may be unrewarding, the objects of her devotion may move far away or die. Any of these experiences will expose the unmet contract, a contract that neither partner may have been conscious of making. Any of these events will give rise to a sense of betrayal. Believing, however incorrectly, that editing and confining herself will lead to intimate connections that will make her feel special, a woman in this situation feels cheated when the connection is broken. And this sense of betrayal is, of course, more intense when real cheating (that is, infidelity) voids the contract. If the fantasy has been something like "If I make myself the perfect partner (wife, mother), I will be rewarded with intimacy. That will make me feel special, worthy, and whole," then to have that fantasy shattered by another, presumably more perfect partner, is especially devastating.

Many women who have lived by this fantasy contract wake up when it is broken. Some appear to wake up and then are drawn back into contract, as perhaps Hannah Arendt was. The breaking of the contract leads to feelings of intense worthlessness, fears of being the wrong kind of person, for if they were the right kind of woman all would be well in the relationship. Still others see their feelings of betrayal and emptiness as the exclusive fault of the object of their devotion, the one who has failed to repay their devotion. As such, these excruciating feelings are channeled into a self-righteous reversal. It is the betrayer who is worthless, who is the wrong kind of person. The intolerable pain of having given up the self for a fantasy contract, of having suppressed one's own individuation for a payoff that will never come, is not used to motivate self-understanding, to focus finally on individuation. Instead, the fantasy must be vindicated through the punishment of the betrayer. If it can be proven that he is in the wrong, then the sacrifice will still be meaningful. The effort made for intimacy was righteous, but the other person was unworthy of that righteous effort. The inauthentic one is out there, not here, inside me. Revenge may take the form of trying to make sure that everyone—family, friends, children, court—knows who is the good person and who is the bad. Or it may go beyond character assassination to legal and extra-legal attack.

The most common form of revenge seems to come through relationships. The intimate refuge is withdrawn and replaced by an intimate persecution. The custody of children, the goodwill of friends and family seem to be the areas in which most vengeful women operate. Claire Bloom's book could be seen as a version of this, taken to a meta-level.[11] Revenge is sought where the woman has power—through emotion, nurturance, children, social life. The broken contract, the uncompensated sacrifice of self, gives the woman victim status in her eyes and in the eyes of some others. Victim status then confers a right to vindication. Vindication is sought in the arena where the sacrifice was made—relationships. Honesty, sensitivity, loyalty, and attention to the interests of others may all go by the wayside for a time. History is revised. This was the clear intent of the famous television interview given by Diana, Princess of Wales, in which she revealed the shadow side of her marriage. Her version of the demise of the "fairy tale marriage" was radically different from the Palace's official history and she wanted her version to prevail in the minds and hearts of her public. Diana and the Prince of Wales were soon in a public relations war, contesting the moral high ground. The Princess sought vindication through her relationship with the public, even though that relationship had been one of the aspects of her life that oppressed her. Her revenge on Prince Charles was, for a time, complete.

I don't believe revenge, in any form, is justifiable. Understandable, perhaps, but neither useful nor healthy. However, when the fantasy contract is broken many women feel that they have been oppressed. Some realize that they have been enslaved to a role, the role of relationship magician, maintainer of intimacy. Others conclude that they have been enslaved by an individual, the betraying partner. Both views have some truth. The role was not constructed by the partner, but the partner, by enacting his own role, has helped to maintain it. Feeling enslaved, many women feel drawn to the necessarily clandestine stratagems of the enslaved, including covert revenge. For this reason, underhanded revenge strategies, such as trying to poison a child's mind against a father, may seem justifiable to a woman who feels powerless.

Our culture validates both the desire for vengeance and the behavior of seeking vengeance, at least in our popular stories. (Revenge is a major part of the plot in most movies.) Either by triumphing in the courtroom or stalking their betrayer, in American narratives the righteously injured resolve their rage and disappointment through legal or extra-legal revenge. Typically, revenge is seen as the appropriate resolution of betrayal and injury; it is the way that our heroes handle their wounded feelings. Betrayal is experienced as a humiliation, especially when it results from the action of a loved one. Feeling "like a fool" is the most common response to being deceived. But revenge is yet another fantasy, a fantasy in which making the betrayer suffer will alleviate his victim's suffering, a fantasy in which destroying the betrayer will destroy the feelings of humiliation and worthlessness that follow betrayal. The outer face of the revenge fantasy is that vengeance will eliminate the humiliation and shame the victim feels. It doesn't.

Medea's vindictive holocaust is meant to erase the false, shameful image of herself as a discardable, dismissable wife.

Medea's attempt to connect her world to Jason's world has failed, her development has stalled, her identity within the marriage is stagnant. When Jason's actions make this obvious, she initiates a new start, detaching from the old identity by annihilating it. For when Medea seeks revenge on Jason, his new love, and all who support them, she is sweeping away their image (and her own?) of herself as a woman who can be treated with contempt. Her quest for a meaningful relationship with Jason has failed, with all that the quest implied. She refuses responsibility for that failure. Since Jason has made the failure obvious, or conscious, she treats him as its only cause. The shadow of her quest is projected onto Jason and all who are associated with him. She attempts to deal with that shadow by trying to destroy it as she perceives it in others, outside herself.

SHADOW PROJECTION

That women habitually use their relationship skills and their dedication to intimacy (relationship magic) to maintain relationships that have little or no basis in true compatibility is the shadow side of the female gift for facilitating relationships. Women who have lived by the "sacrificing-myself-to-relationships-will-make-me-special" contract encounter that shadow when that contract is broken. The impersonal, exploitive nature of such relationships becomes obvious. Seeking revenge on the contract breaker is a sign that this encounter with the shadow is being dealt with through projection. The partner who was carrying the animus projection, who was the mirror in which the woman sought her true image, now carries the shadow of the quest for intimacy.

Cora told me of a revenge fantasy she had. In this fantasy, she would aggressively confront and destroy various comfortable notions her former partner had about their past relationship, effectively replacing his understanding with her own view. Needless to say, her view of her partner's behavior was considerably more critical than his own. This was a very mild revenge, compared to Medea's, and Cora never acted on the fantasy. Such fantasies are widespread, certainly more widespread than actual attempts at revenge. To some extent, they represent the last vestige of one of the most powerful intimate desires—the desire to be understood. The quest for mirroring and recognition, so important in intimacy and so elusive for women, goes on even after the relationship is over, in imagination. But this kind of fantasy also represents an attempt to settle the shadow of the quest for intimacy onto the missing partner.

Every person has a shadow and every culture has a shadow. Women are carrying American culture's shadow in the realm of relationships. Previously I have described this collective shadow as baggage being carried by the quest for intimacy. Jean Baker Miller has described this baggage as unsolved aspects of human experience. As I quoted her in chapter three: "women, then, become the 'carriers' of those aspects of the total human experience that remain unsolved . . . these parts of experience have been removed from the arena of full and open interchange and relegated increasingly to a realm outside of full awareness, in which they take on all sorts of frightening attributes."[12]

Women carry the unsolved aspects of human relationships, in other words the shadow of intimacy, for their partners and for culture at large. In carrying the collective shadow and trying to fix it through individual action, women feel simultaneously scapegoated and anointed. "Being needed because one is inferior or hateful or loathsome is deeply felt by many women. . . . Women have generally carried, along with minority groups, the collective shadow of heroic Western consciousness. . . . Glorified by themselves and the collective [society] as chosen ones, and equally despised as illicit, alien, second class and victim, they are too often the silent and patient vessels of necessary but derogated shadow qualities."[13]

Acts of betrayal, like Jason's, are apt to shatter "silent and patient vessels." The silence and patience have been supported by the expectation of a payoff, the fulfillment of the fantasy contract: "I will carry this shadow for you and my sacrifice, how ever awful and empty it feels, will be rewarded." When the sacrifice is not rewarded, the shadow is out of the vessel and looking for a home. The woman may take it on as a reflection of herself, saying, in essence, "My quest failed because I am unlovable, unworthy"—the Pope would apparently agree with her here—or she may rebel against the pain of that by giving the shadow a home in her past partner. This is the psychological dynamic that underlies a movement, as we saw in Princess Diana's actions, from the self-hating behaviors of suicidal gestures or bulimia to the vengeful behaviors of retaliatory affairs and public character attacks. When the fantasy dies, the shadow of the quest for intimacy is first experienced as a devastating self-image and then is projected onto the partner.

This shadow projection is not hard to maintain because men often seem to behave very badly in relationships. The shadow that men carry as relationship partners is one we have touched on in our previous discussion of Bluebeard. Our collective perception of men in relationships partakes heavily of this shadow—ranging from a fairly mild "men-are-dogs" stance to a perception of men as generally dangerous.[14] If a woman has taken on an impossible partner, including taking on his hoped-for transformation as a part of her search for meaningful relationships, then she has taken on the masculine shadow in relationship. Her shadow, springing from the promiscuous use of relationship magic, and his, springing from the exploitation of women in intimate relationships, are in a sense mated. The end of Bluebeard's story may tell us something about that connection.

As you recall, Bluebeard's wife has discovered his secret, forbidden room, full of the dismembered bodies of his past wives. Returning from a business trip, Bluebeard realizes that his wife has been in the room.

"You must die, madam," said he, "and that presently."

"If I must die," she said, "give me some time to say my prayers."

"I give you a quarter of an hour."

She spent that quarter hour anxiously looking out for the arrival of her brothers, who had intended to come that day. At last, just as she saw their dust on the road, her husband came in. Taking hold of her hair, he lifted his sword, intending to take her head while she implored him for her life. At this very instant, a loud knocking at the gate caused Bluebeard to stop. His wife's brothers, one a musketeer and the other a dragoon, rushed in with drawn swords. Chasing Bluebeard down, they ran him through and left him dead.[15]

Bluebeard does not just tell us about a masculine shadow aspect, but about the connection between it and a feminine shadow as it is manifested in a relationship. The feminine shadow comes out as a tendency to pursue intimacy without adequate attention to the issue of compatibility and to the suffering that incompatibility causes both partners, just as Bluebeard's wife ignores the obvious problems and marries him anyway. The masculine shadow is the tendency to use intimacy as a convenience, and the intimate partner as an object of use, just as Bluebeard is willing to dispatch any wife who does not behave perfectly. The feminine shadow makes it possible for the masculine shadow to thrive. The masculine shadow in these relationships is so obvious that it gives the feminine shadow cover. After all, if men are dogs, do we have to look any farther than that for the truth of a failed relationship or for the justification of female vengeance? After all, a vengeful woman is just doing what was done to her, a process that therapists call "passive-into-active transference."[16]

Symbolically, Bluebeard must die before anything else can happen. The interlocked connection between the feminine and masculine relationship shadows must be broken. Only this makes it possible for a woman to stop carrying the collective shadow of negative Eros, to stop projecting her own shadow onto the impossible partner and come back to attending to her own individuation. In one relationship that Cora had, she felt seduced by her partner's spiritual authority (an authority that was quite real), so that she idealized him. This meant that she was carrying his shadow in the relationship; he was so perfect that all of the problems must certainly be in her. As she described it, "I was wrestling with the shadow, I was on the mat, the unacknowledged shadow side almost did me in."

Cora went through a crisis in which she suffered through a number of psychosomatic illnesses, until she finally acknowledged the problematic nature of this relationship. Cora said, "My expertise in working things out with him and my resilient hope about the potential of the relationship were hooked to something destructive." Cora was using her command of relationship magic to maintain an inauthentic relationship in which she was, on some level, being exploited. The shadow of her gift for facilitating relationships made fertile ground for her partner's shadow. In her quest for intimacy, and the special development she hoped it would hold for her, she recklessly ignored her partner's real character. This was also Medea's folly.

CHAPTER SIX

Why the Search Fails

MEDEA flew from Corinth in a chariot drawn by winged dragons, steeds sprung from the Titans. First she flew to Thebes where she cured Heracles of the madness which had caused him to kill his children. Having killed the Theban princess that Jason had wanted to marry, she could not stay in Thebes but flew on to Athens. The king there, Aegeus, had sworn to shelter her if she was ever in need. He and Medea married. She lived in Athens until she was accused of attempting to poison Theseus, the heir to the throne. She traveled to Thessaly and Italy, where she is still worshipped as a goddess. She lived for a time in Asia Minor, where she was rumored to have married a king. Finally returning to Colchis with her son, whose father may have been Jason or may have been the Asian king, she helped her father regain his throne.

Jason, meanwhile, wandered homeless, cursed by the gods for dishonoring their names when he broke his oath to Medea. In old age, he came once more to Corinth and sat down in the shadow of the prow of the *Argo*, remembering past glories and thinking of the disasters that had overwhelmed him. Suddenly, the wreck toppled forward and killed him. Medea never died but became immortal. She reigns in the Elysian fields, that part of the underworld where the virtuous are eternally content, unless they choose to be reborn.

Medea's quest continues, and continues to fail. Eventually she returns to her starting place, Colchis. Like Circe, she retreats to her sacred grove. At story's end, she is completely removed from mainstream consciousness, ruling over the Elysian Fields, the Greek underworld Valhalla of worthy heroes. Ultimately her quest was folly. Her effort to make a bridge between her world and the dominant world order has failed. Medea does not find a viable way to connect to patriarchal Greece. As one mythographer puts it, "From Colchis to Thessaly to Corinth to Athens to Persia she flees, unable to take root in the Greek mythic landscape."[1] She cannot find a place in a world dominated by Logos, by patriarchal values. Medea attempts to find a place in the mainstream, she fails, she moves on. She does this a number of times, recreating her experience with Jason in less dramatic versions. Out in the world at large, there is no place for her sensibility that does not suppress that sensibility, no setting in which the meaning of her quest can come to fruition. She returns to the enclosed world of her childhood, Colchis. Her fate is both ancient and contemporary. The personal, emotional, and spiritual truth of women's lives has not, even now, found a secure place to take root in the Western world's landscape. The female quest for intimacy, framed as an attempt to develop the authentic self and connect it to the world, seems to fail, more often than not.

In one of our conversations, Cora was comparing one of her relationships to another when she suddenly said, "Oh my God, I only just realized, I did the same thing in the next relationship, even though I was sure I wasn't going to. It's so embarrassing." Both parts of her statement are important, both the sense of repeating an experience and the sense of shame. Repeated, futile effort to fulfill the quest for intimacy may occur within one relationship or across several. Typically we understand these repeated failures as personal failures, so we feel shame. As we have already discussed, failure in intimacy is experienced by women as a flaw in the self. Some may frame it as a moral flaw ("if I were good enough, I would be loved enough"); some, as a physical flaw ("if I were beautiful enough, I would be lovable"); some, as a psychological flaw ("if only I weren't so neurotic, I would have the intimate relationship I need").

Doing the same thing again and again, while believing that, sometime, it will turn out differently, is a good colloquial definition of neurosis. By that definition, women who try again and again are neurotic.[2] Psychologists tend to assume that such a pattern springs from conflicts that originated in childhood and are being unconsciously recreated in adulthood. They, too, see it as an individual, personal problem. But it is more than that. Of course, the disappointments that women suffer in their quest for intimacy are personal and have personal roots. However, those personal roots are completely intertwined with larger issues. The family each woman grew up in was shaped by the same cultural factors that impact that woman's adult life. As feminists have been telling us for thirty years, the personal is political. The personal is also societal, cultural, and archetypal.

I have suggested in previous chapters that in their quest for intimacy, women may be carrying considerable baggage. While women are personally seeking relationships that will allow them to realize their inner world in an authentic way (a way denied to them by the culture at large), they may also be grappling with a collective problem by seeking to re-enchant life for themselves and their loved ones, to make a meaningful home in a disenchanted world, embodying feminine values in a culture that denies those values. In attempting to bridge the divide between inner experience and outer reality, individual women are taking on a more than personal problem. When pursuing their individuation through relationships, women are confronted by deep splits that are cultural, religious, and philosophical in nature, splits that are, at the root, collective rather than individual.

Our polarizations of autonomy and togetherness, self and relationship, culture and nature, profoundly affect the female quest for intimacy. A masculinized collective ego ideal, emphasizing autonomy, competition, invulnerability, and transcendence, supports the value of rising above the physical, everyday world while shadowy, unrecognized feminine values support the effort to make a home in that world. As a consequence, women carry an unsolved problem on the spiritual level—the problem of the Western world's alienation from nature and Eros and the difficulty of establishing a sense of "at-homeness" for oneself and one's family in a disenchanted world. Through personal action, women have taken on, albeit in an unarticulated and, for the most part, unconscious way, the effort to ameliorate a number of inter-related, deeply conflicted issues that spring from the dualism of Western culture. Medea's quest can be seen as an attempt to bridge this duality at its beginning place in history.

Bianca, while describing the struggles that came up in a long-distance relationship, touched on the internal conflict that accompanies an attempt to bridge opposites in relationship: "It came down to this— 'Can I be who I am now and accommodate to who he is?' I was willing to work with that, but it seemed that he could not. He could not accommodate to what I was becoming. And I thought, in that case, we can't work on this. I have to admit that I occasionally thought, 'I could change him,' but then I would think, 'That sucks.' So mostly, for that year and a half I kept coming back to, 'Can I live with this?' I would rationalize, 'Oh, it's the stress of the circumstances.' Within the framework of the decisions we were making (decisions about who would change job and location), I have to say that, if there was going to be a compromise, it would have had to come from me, I would have to change. That was implicit."

Something we see in Medea's story is that, even if the woman is willing to change completely, as Medea did while she was married to Jason, the quest fails. Robert Graves calls Medea's post-Jason life, "Medea in Exile," but, in fact, she was in exile while married—exiled from her own path. In the aftermath of her marriage to Jason, her most spectacular folly, she has adventures in Thebes, Athens, Italy, Thessaly, Asia Minor, all preludes to retreat. She searches for recognition, for place. Her persistence is striking. At the beginning of this book, I wrote that I am both amazed and impatient when I observe women's capacity for love and what appears to be their capacity for poor judgment. In my psychotherapy practice, in my friendships, in my students, in reading Hannah Arendt's letters, I see women trying, again and again, to achieve intimacy, true intimacy, almost an exalted intimacy. They quest to attain the unattainable, to find something ineffably precious that, even if found, cannot be held. In this, they are engaged in a truly mythic endeavor. Unfortunately, many, perhaps most, do not see this journey as mythic and symbolic. They see it as concrete, the fantasy contract by which they will achieve a sense of being special and lovable.

A quest requires an object, a precious and meaningful goal. However, the most important thing about a quest is not the object being sought. It is the effect the journey has on the seeker. This is a common insight, but no less true for its familiarity. The quest's fundamental purpose is revealed in the way that it changes the quester. Psychologically, quests are stories about the self, the self's development and place in the world. In stories about the knights of the Round Table and their quest for the Holy Grail, the knights find out who they really are while they are searching. They encounter haunted woods, sorcerers, enchanted maidens, and disappearing castles. All of these obstacles and tests are, in the psychological terms of the quest, opportunities for different aspects of each knight's self to emerge. The fact that only one knight achieves the end of the quest and finds the Grail is not important. All who participated found out something vital about themselves. Turning again to Diana, Princess of Wales, we can see that, although her quest to have meaningful intimacy in her marriage failed, the ups and downs of that quest led her to know herself and to make a meaningful life for herself in her work with AIDS patients and the land-mine removal project.

I have postulated that the psychological point of this journey for women lies in their effort to connect a uniquely feminine inner world to a masculinized outer world. The quest for intimacy is an effort to develop and preserve the authentic self, at the same time connecting that self, through the partner, to the world at large, a world that tends to treat the feminine as trivial or pathological. If a woman is able to fulfill this course of individuation through her quest, she has fulfilled its psychological purpose, *regardless of the specific outcome* of a specific relationship. So when Cora, Lauren, and Bianca reflect on what they have learned in the past about themselves and about the nature of their relationships they are describing the psychological rewards of the quest for us.

Lauren described both the dedication of the questing spirit and the conflict that the quest encompasses in this way: "With women, there's the sense of doing everything to support the relationship. Women have an investment in coming to conclusions about relationships that make you stay connected to your partner. It's weighted in that direction. There's a gigantic difference between men and women. Men don't hold the hearth." The gigantic difference between men and women is fueled and maintained, at least in part by the fact that women are trying to bridge collective opposites with personal action, trying to grapple with the splitting of experience by their culture through pursuing a certain kind of intimacy.

Lauren continued to describe her experience of polarization in relationship: "There's a lot of giving up the self with women, so much nurturance to the relationship as an entity. You definitely hold that consciousness, you are engaged on the project of 'what will make the relationship work.' It can be codependent. Attending to the self is seen as not being connected—it's somehow bad. Togetherness is the highest value for women, but our society is flipped out in the other direction. Socially, independence is the best thing, connection is an accident. We haven't achieved a balance. Men go out and follow the dream of independence. Women have the conflict, how can they be whole people, go out and work, do what's important to them, and at the same time be good wives and mommies? Men don't seem to even care to try to be whole in that way. When I was married, I wrestled with this question all the time, every day. How do I make this decision? I want to stay in the library and read, but I'm married, so I'm not supposed to. We don't seem to have worked out an overt way to hold all the pieces—to say, 'Yes, I'm married, and I am going to make this simple decision about how to spend the evening by myself.' As with any split, we must find a way to live with both sides, to hold both sides, both pieces. It's a dichotomy."

As we have seen, this dichotomy springs from and depends on a number of other dichotomies. Not only are women seeking to gain recognition for their own authentic selves in relationships but they are also engaged, in this most personal side of life, with the fundamental contradictions of their culture. This engagement goes on, for the most part, without support or guidance, because the contradictions are not consciously acknowledged. When Lauren was wrestling with her everyday questions in the library, she was grappling with the unacknowledged shadow of the quest for intimacy. It is that shadow which most often deters women from realizing the psychological benefits of their quest.

As we discussed, in carrying the collective shadow and trying to fix it through individual action, women feel simultaneously scapegoated and anointed. Returning to Perera's cogent description, we are reminded that women are "glorified by themselves and the collective [society] as chosen ones, and equally despised as illicit, alien, second class and victim, they are too often the silent and patient vessels of necessary but derogated shadow qualities."[3] The necessary shadow qualities being carried by women in the quest for intimacy are need, vulnerability, normal dependency, emotionality, and surrender to nature, especially as experienced in the body. By holding these shadow qualities, women compensate for and balance the dominant collective ego ideal, making it possible for that ideal to continue unquestioned. This amounts to a collective form of codependency and gives women a painful way to be special, indispensable.

By holding these shadow qualities, women also place themselves in a psychologically dangerous position. The most persistent dangers in a woman's quest for intimacy lie in the woman's beliefs, both conscious and unconscious. The following beliefs make it difficult for women to develop the resources, inner or outer, that will sustain them in a crisis: the belief that attending to the self is inherently opposed to attending to relationships; the belief that expressing love for a partner and assessing the compatibility of a partner are mutually exclusive; the belief that all problems in a relationship are the woman's problems. The notion that women are responsible for the behavior of their partners is an outcome of these beliefs. Thus difficulties with the partner are experienced as a problem *within the self,* a personal shadow issue, not as an interpersonal dilemma.

A woman who believes these things is likely to respond to a crisis in a relationship by struggling to perfect herself, to make herself into a more worthy, lovable partner, rather than by trying to understand the problem as mutual and interactive. Some women develop anorexic or bulimic eating disorders, as Princess Diana did, struggling to perfect their bodies as a way of addressing relationship problems. These are the convictions and reactions that fix a woman in the role of relationship magician, whether she is a saintly one or a witchy one. The fantasy contract in which one exchanges one's own path for the feeling of specialness continues to dominate individuation, even when the contract is a manifest failure. Staying stuck in that contract prevents a woman from learning from the journey. This can go on until something explodes, until something irrefutable happens that shatters the inauthentic facade of the relationship. At that point, the woman's self-blame may intensify, or it may reverse and be vengefully projected onto the partner. Either way she is stuck in a battle with the shadow of intimacy.

The shadow of intimacy, in a typical heterosexual relationship, results from the mating of a masculine shadow and a feminine shadow. The feminine shadow comes out as a tendency to pursue intimacy without adequate attention to the issue of compatibility and to the suffering that incompatibility causes both partners. So Medea ignores Jason's manifest character and, later, punishes him for being who he has been all along. Bluebeard's wife ignores the obvious problems with Bluebeard's reputation and marries him anyway. The masculine shadow is the tendency to use intimacy as a convenience, and the intimate partner as an object of use. So Jason can't imagine that his wife might make infidelity hard on him and Bluebeard is willing to dispatch any wife who does not behave perfectly. The feminine shadow makes it possible for the masculine shadow to thrive. The masculine shadow allows the feminine shadow to appear selfless.

Linguistic research brings this dynamic into specific focus. Linguist Deborah Tannen finds that most women use conversational strategies that seek rapport. For instance, many women will strive to find *something* in another person's statement that they can agree with, even if they disagree with the overall gist of the statement, and will emphasize the instance of agreement rather than the general disagreement. This approach tends to be perceived by others as an expression of powerlessness.[4] A woman's emphasis on points of agreement may be read as a lack of interest in asserting her own opinion and a willingness to adopt the other's opinion. Since men's conversational strategies tend to seek power, a tragic misunderstanding can take place in which continued striving for rapport by a female partner may be misread as an invitation to domination by a male partner. I think that the unconscious conversational strategies that Tannen uncovers in her analyses of conversations are expressions of the shadow material that comes out in the quest for intimacy. In conversation the feminine shadow seeks to produce an experience of rapport without knowing if real compatibility exists; the masculine shadow seeks an experience of control, without acknowledging the effect of domination on the partner.

When a woman is unconsciously beset with the drive to produce intimacy, regardless of compatibility, her quest does not transform her. She is obsessed with the goal, at the expense of the process. The process of a quest holds the real potential for transformation. The journey itself, whatever the nature of its twists and turns, provides the opportunity to know and develop the self. However, as long as a woman believes in the dichotomy of self and relationship, believes that intimacy requires the suppression of parts of the authentic self, she will continue to experience those twists and turns as obstacles to her fantasy fulfillment, striving to realize the relationship instead of the self, rather than with the self.

Consequently the archetypal power of the quest motif is distorted. Opportunities to come to terms with her own shadow and her partner's shadow are lost, because she wants only to ignore or get around shadow traits, often using relationship magic to do so. Many women who are caught as shadow carriers appear martyred. Like Claire Bloom in her book, they may actively present themselves that way. Like Hannah Arendt, they may rationalize their behavior, although this does not prevent others from seeing them as victims.

I have described the shadow of intimacy as a union of a feminine shadow and a masculine shadow. I believe these two shadows to be equally problematic, and I believe that, psychologically, they contribute equally to destructive relationships. However, they do not *function* equally. The feminine shadow is actually portrayed, in collective cultural imagery, as positive. The feminine shadow's indiscriminate pursuit of closeness, regardless of the resulting relationship's safety or authenticity, is typically framed as a womanly gift of selfless love. If Hannah Arendt had showed exactly the same level of devotion to an old teacher and lover who had fallen on hard times but whose faults were not public as Heidegger's were, she probably would have been praised for it. No one would have questioned the appropriateness of her actions.

Women are not encouraged to challenge the shadow of their gift for making relationships as it operates within themselves. As we have discussed, they are actually encouraged to believe that being more immersed in the feminine shadow, that is, to give more love without discrimination or assessment, is the path to successful intimacy. Despite the success of books like *Women Who Love Too Much*, the redemptive power of devotion is still constantly proclaimed in women's magazines, movies, novels, television shows, and advice columns. Women who assess a partner's suitability before committing themselves to a relationship are still portrayed as cold, calculating, and destructive.

The masculine shadow, the Bluebeard or Jason figure, meanwhile, is supported by a patriarchal bias toward allowing a man to rule in his own home, his own "castle" (witness O. J. Simpson's famous ability to avoid assault charges for beating up his wife). Society gives lip service to condemning male domestic tyrants while continuing to glorify the desire for mastery and the objectification of women and children that drive such men. The raw, socially accepted power of the masculine shadow, whether that power is physical, economic, or psychological, and the way that it dominates and sometimes destroys those we see as innocent and pure, creates a seeming impasse. The masculine shadow, as it manifests in intimate relationships, begins to seem larger than life, unstoppable. This psychological impasse can make it seem that only a trickster could possibly survive an encounter with such an overwhelming opponent. A woman may come to feel that her choice is to be a victim of intimacy's shadow or a trickster that masters that shadow.

THE TRICKSTER ADAPTATION

From the beginning of her story, Medea is a trickster. She tricks her father, the dragon that guards the fleece, her half-brother, Jason's Uncle Pelias, Jason, and his new bride. Her power and her rage are expressed through sleight of hand. Tricksters are common figures in myth and folklore. Like the Raven of the Pacific Northwest Native mythology, they may use their shapeshifting abilities to get things going, break up stalemates, and make things happen. Like the African-American Bre'r Rabbit, they may be subversive, using their knowledge of the shadow side of life to undermine the authority of those who have power.[5] Medea has both of these effects. So does someone like the comedian Roseanne or the singer/actress Madonna, both of whom take a trickster's stance toward their audiences. Like other female icons, female tricksters carry shadow material. (Roseanne carries the shadow of female anger and appetite for power, Madonna the shadow of female sexual desire and, again, power.) However, tricksters carry shadow material in a very particular way, a way that unsettles the collective ego ideal rather than supports it. They are not enablers, their connection to patriarchal values is disruptive rather than codependent. The trickster's way is a popular image for women right now, one that represents an evolving position for the feminine in culture.

A myth like that of Medea portrays the universal underpinnings, the deep structure, as it were, of a human experience and, as a consequence, such a myth illuminates the meaning of that experience. However, because of this depth, such a myth tends to use imagery that is somewhat distant from daily human life. Medea's choices and actions are powerful metaphors for archetypal potentials, but they do not help us to completely understand the woman who develops a trickster adaptation or to interpret the emergence of the female trickster in popular culture today. Fairy tales, however, might be of more help in the effort to understand. They seem to embody more detailed, everyday human experiences than the more sweeping images of a great myth. A fairy tale is an archetypal story that can mediate between the "otherness" of mythic images and everyday life; it is a mixture of the mundane and the mythic. By looking at a fairy tale about a trickster, we may clothe the deep archetypal structures in specifics of human experience. The following is a variation of the Bluebeard motif, one which I mentioned in the first chapter, called "Fitcher's Bird." Its setup is classic Bluebeard, but its female protagonist is something new, a trickster-wife.

Fitcher's Bird

THERE was once a wizard who used to pretend to be a beggar in order to catch pretty girls. One day he appeared before the door of a man who had three pretty daughters. The wizard carried the eldest away to his house, which stood in the midst of a dark forest. Everything in the house was magnificent; he gave her everything she could possibly desire and said, "My darling, you will certainly be happy with me, for you have everything your heart can desire." This lasted a few days, and then he said: "I must journey forth and leave you alone for a short time. Here are the keys of the house. You may go everywhere and look at everything except into one room, which this little key opens, and there I forbid you to go." He likewise gave her an egg and said, "Preserve the egg carefully for me, and carry it continually about with you."

The young woman took the egg and promised to obey him in everything. When he was gone, she went all around the house from the bottom to the top and examined everything. The rooms shone with silver and gold, and she thought she had never seen such great splendor. At length she came to the forbidden door, and though she wanted to be obedient, she could have no rest until she went in. But what did she see when she entered? A great bloody basin stood in the middle of the room, and therein lay women's bodies, dead and hewn to pieces. She was so terribly alarmed that the egg, which she held in her hand, fell into the basin. She washed and scrubbed, but she could not get the blood off the egg.

It was not long before the wizard returned from his journey, and the first things he asked for were the key and the egg. She gave them to him, but she trembled as she did so, and he saw at once by the red spots that she had been in the bloody chamber. "Since you have gone into the room against my will," said he, "you shall go back into it against your own. Your life is ended." He threw her down, dragged her along by her hair, cut off her head on the block, and hewed her in pieces so that her blood ran on the ground.

Then he went back for the second daughter. He caught her like the first, by simply touching her, and then he carried her away. She did not fare better than her sister. Then the wizard went and brought the third sister, but she was wily. When he had given her the keys and the egg and had left, she put the egg away with great care and then examined the house, going at last into the forbidden room. Both her sisters were in the bloody basin, cruelly murdered and cut in pieces. But she began to gather their limbs together and put them in order—head, body, arms, and legs. When nothing further was wanting, the limbs began to move and unite themselves together, and both the maidens were once more alive. Then they rejoiced and kissed and held one another.

The wizard returned and at once demanded the keys and the egg. When he could perceive no trace of any blood on the egg, he said, "You have passed the test, you shall be my bride." He no longer had any power over her; rather, he was forced to do whatever she desired. Said she, "You shall first take a basketful of gold to my father and mother, and carry it yourself on your back. In the meantime, I will prepare for the wedding." Then she ran to her sisters, whom she had hidden in a little chamber, and said, "The time has come when I can save you. The wretch himself shall take you home again, but as soon as you are at home, send help."

She put both of them in a basket and covered them

over with gold, so that nothing of them was to be seen. Then she called in the wizard and said to him, "Now carry the basket away, but I shall look through my little window and watch to see if you stop." The wizard raised the basket on his back and went away with it, but it weighed him down so heavily that the sweat streamed from his face. Then he sat down to rest. But immediately one of the girls in the basket cried, "I am looking through my little window, and I see that you are resting. Go on at once!" He thought it was his bride talking to him, and he got up on his legs again. And whenever he stood still, she cried this, and then he was forced to go onward, until at last, groaning and out of breath, he took the basket with the gold and the two maidens into their parents' house.

At home the bride prepared the marriage feast and sent invitations to the friends of the wizard. Then she took a skull with grinning teeth, put some ornaments and a wreath of flowers on it, carried it upstairs to the garret window, and let it look out from thence. When all was ready, she got into a barrel of honey and then cut the feather-bed open and rolled herself in it, until she looked like a wondrous bird, and no one could recognize her. Then she went out of the house, and on her way she met some of the wedding guests, who asked,

"O, Fitcher's bird, how com'st thou here?"
"I come from Fitcher's house quite near."
"And what may the young bride be doing?"
"From cellar to garret she's swept all clean,
And now from the window she's peeping, I ween."
At last she met the bridegroom, who was coming

slowly back. He, like the others asked,

"O, Fitcher's bird, how com'st thou here?"
"I come from Fitcher's house quite near."
"And what may the young bride be doing?"
"From cellar to garret she's swept all clean,
And now from the window she's peeping, I ween."

The bridegroom looked up, saw the decked-out skull, thought it was his bride, and nodded to her, greeting her kindly. When he and all his guests had arrived, the bride's kinsmen, sent by her sisters, locked the doors of the house and set fire to it. The wizard and all his crew had to burn.[6]

The third sister, like Medea, is a trickster. Jung describes the archetypal trickster as having "a fondness for sly jokes, and miraculous pranks, power as a shape shifter, a dual nature, part animal, a tendency to expose himself to torture and an approximation to the figure of a savior."[7] We can easily see these traits in the third daughter. She is sly, as evidenced by her trick with the egg. Her pranks include fooling the wizard into laboriously carrying her sisters home and dressing up the skeleton as a bride. The wily sister pretends to be willing to marry the wizard and to prepare for a wedding she does not intend to complete. She is a shape-shifter who appears as an animal, the bird made of honey and feathers. She is in danger of torture and death throughout the story, and she is her sisters' savior. She gives us a humanized version of Medea's tricky ways.

Tricksters are cultural outsiders. They manifest an extreme version of the outsider's double consciousness, what

Jung calls a "dual nature." The tricksterish tendency to shape-shift is both a protective covering for a person with limited power and a transformative potential developed in secret.[8] This allows a woman to outwardly accommodate a confining cultural role while preserving a private, secret inner life; it allows the third sister to avoid annihilation by appearing compliant while holding onto a hidden ability to make her own choices. Her capacity for maintaining both stances at once is her dual nature, and is a fundamental requirement of being a successful trickster. This story differs from other versions of Bluebeard, because the wily sister refuses to limit her consciousness in the way that the wizard demands, i.e., she silently and *consciously* reserves the right to decide where to carry the egg, what room to enter. She does not strive to be loved, recognized, or understood by being good, compliant, and lovable. She strives only to best the wizard.

The female trickster escapes the double bind of the female gender role, the bind that simultaneously surrounds women with a glorious mystique and a scathing contempt. The pervasive double bind—to be a good woman is to fail at the culture's ego ideal and thus to be contemptible, to attain the culture's ego ideal is to be a bad woman—does not hold the trickster because she does not quest for intimacy. The third sister is not looking for someone to help, to be a muse or confidante to, nor is she looking for flattery, seduction, or love. She is not trying to connect her inner world to the outer world through a partner. She is trying to protect that inner world, keep it secret and safe from the masculine shadow, the Bluebeard/wizard.

The third sister is the first, and in the life of the story the only family member, to become aware of the wizard's shadow nature yet remain alive; that is, symbolically speaking, she is the only one to remain conscious of the grim reality. As soon as the first two sisters encounter the shadow, they are overwhelmed by it and die. Consequently, the wily sister is the only one who has the opportunity to save her sisters from the masculine shadow. Jung says, regarding the trickster as savior, "[T]he recognition and unavoidable integration of the shadow creates such a harrowing situation that nobody but a savior can undo the tangled web of fate."[9] The female trickster has eschewed the injunction to "not know" absorbed by most normally socialized women. When pubescent girls, as documented by Gilligan's research, are learning to obscure their sense of "knowing," somehow the trickster hangs onto hers. Unlike her sisters, she is good at protecting herself and maintains an excellent facade, until the moment she chooses to come out.

The trickster's secret acts of defiance help her preserve a sense of internal independence and identity. The wily sister puts the egg safely aside, even though at this point in the story she cannot know its significance. This is a conscious gesture of resistance. She chooses to disobey rather than trying to be good and then giving in to a compulsive, unconscious rebellion, such as the impulse that overwhelms her compliant sisters and causes them to enter the forbidden room. These conscious gestures are crucial. They preserve an inner spark of autonomy and represent the refusal to bond completely with the aggressor.

The first two sisters seem to represent the persistent fantasy that placating the masculine shadow is the best, safest route and that being good will transform a dangerous situation. They try to be obedient and failing that, apologetic. This is a child's notion of how to ward off danger. Women's frequent, infantile fantasy is that to bond with the aggressor will change him. Once again, the Beauty, through the gift of love, will supposedly transform any Beast. This is not a fantasy that individual, misguided women have come up with. It is pervasive and culturally endorsed. The female trickster plays with this fantasy, using the assumptions of others, especially men, that she is following the usual path as a cover for her own power plays. Think of Mae West's aura of superfeminine parody, masking both a skeptic's view of male importance and a strategy for her own betterment.

I have used extreme figures—Madonna, Roseanne, Mae West—as examples. Of course, most women do not adopt such obvious trickster poses. Instead, we more typically see a movement from sincere devotion to a relationship to the incorporation of tricksterish behaviors. Someone like Diana, Princess of Wales, might begin by having separate friends, with whom she enjoys "disloyal" conversations, progressing to secret affairs and to press manipulation. Eventually, Diana was able to leave her marriage, while simultaneously preserving the position it had given her—a move any trickster would be proud of.

By deliberately safeguarding an inner sense of choice and her own right to "know," the female trickster preserves an internal reflective space that is not dominated by the image of what a good woman should do. Her inner life is not run by guilt, shame, or yearning, and so she has room within, mental space, in which to come to her own conclusions. She can act, rather than react, and in this way she seems connected to her animus. At the very least, she does not project the animus, with its power to mediate between inner experience and role demands, onto the wizard. However, because she is covert she can seem cynical, inauthentic. A recent book called *The Rules*, in which the female authors suggest a protocol of behaviors that will manipulate men into commitment, seems to be to be an excellent example of this.[10] The authors do not recommend dedication, love, sincerity, or goodness as a path to establishing intimacy. They recommend keeping your true feelings to yourself and doing what works to get what you want from overbearing and recalcitrant males. In these ways, the trickster is excellent at thwarting the domineering masculine shadow, but that is not enough. Other parts of the self must be reborn if her well-protected inner world is not to atrophy.

The trickster is accompanied in life by a hidden side, represented in "Fitcher's Bird" by the dismembered, innocent, trusting, and powerless sisters, trapped in the bloody chamber. The sisters reflect an important part of the trickster's psyche, the part which holds potential for authentic individuation. The sisters' fate also symbolizes the dismemberment of the feminine by the domination of certain cultural values. The first two sisters in "Fitcher's Bird" represent a kind of innocence that cannot survive in a place like the wizard's castle, a childlike approach to relationships that is an invitation to the masculine shadow. The sisters enter into an unconscious agreement to limit their own awareness, they agree to not know, to avoid looking in the forbidden room. They give over the power to determine reality to the wizard, as they might to a parent. The animus functions of self-protection and relying on one's own perception are projected onto the wizard: he will determine if they are safe, he will dictate good and bad. They represent a particularly extreme, regressed version of the feminine shadow of intimacy.

The sisters' captivity in the wizard's castle personifies the entrapped mating of the feminine shadow and the masculine shadow. Their dismemberment is a necessary symbolic event. Dismemberment, as we have seen in Medea's Cauldron of Regeneration, is a common precursor to transformation. Dismemberment can be interpreted as symbolizing the deconstruction of an existing stance towards life, a stance that has proven unworkable. However, the first two sisters do not return from dismemberment through their own development. In order to reclaim the full potential of the self, the trickster must visit the bloody chamber. She must reassemble the dismembered sisters, who cannot participate with individuation until she shows up.

All three sisters, taken together, symbolize various parts of the self. The wily sister represents a conscious part of the self. She portrays an ego that is approaching relationships with a trickster's stance. The dismembered sisters represent the vulnerable, innocent feelings that have been wounded and shut away in response to danger and exploitation. When the ego learns to handle the danger, in this case through a trickster strategy, it is possible to resurrect the more vulnerable parts of the self, represented here by the dismembered sisters.

After the sisters are reborn, the wily sister fools the wizard into believing that she has obeyed him. At this point, his wizard's power begins to change hands; he must do what his bride-to-be asks him to do. Psychologically, this symbolizes a stage in which a woman begins to set her own terms in life. This aspect of her animus is no longer being projected onto a man. Its important to notice that the sisters, and the trusting feelings they symbolize, still must be protected from the masculine shadow; they must be gotten safely home before the denouement, the deconstruction of the masculine shadow and the transformation of the trickster, can take place.

The path to transformation for the wily sister begins with an egg. Putting away the egg instead of following orders and carrying it around with her is her first act of independent awareness. Her path continues with exploration and the discovery of the dismembered parts of the self, the sisters. Those parts are reanimated, and the power of the animus is used to bring them home, back into consciousness. Awareness of the true nature of things continues to be expressed when the third sister dresses the skeleton as a bride. She is the one who finally realizes that all of the wizard's brides are corpses, that all unions of the masculine shadow with the feminine shadow end in loss of consciousness.

Finally the trickster fulfills the promise of the egg and finds freedom as a wondrous bird. The egg symbolizes the potential for true self-development, a potential that persists even under deep shadow. The wondrous and magical quality of the third sister's exit from the wizard's domain, as a huge singing bird, reflects the power of the evolving self. The creative energy of the unconscious allows her to be artful and humorous in her response to events. The imagery of honey and feathers flaunts the freedom and joy of the emerging self, making the third sister seem almost like a performance artist.

Speaking of the trickster archetype, theorist Ron Messer states, "The Trickster can serve as a gateway back to the revivifying aspects of the unconscious, which can renew and regenerate conscious life."[11] The wily sister is working with the unconscious, and seems to be in an intermediate, transitional stage. Working with the unconscious is essentially an alchemical process, cyclical not linear, where dualistic categories blend, and many splits are bridged. The unconscious is a storehouse of transformative images and the trickster works with those images, transforming one thing into another, body parts into living sister, a wizard into a servant, a skeleton into a bride, herself into a bird. She is operating at the threshold between the mundane and the mythic, in a twilight world. It is not "a sharply circumscribed world with clear forms but a consciousness of imagination . . . an intermediate realm between bright, clear, daylight and pitch-black night; the mediumistic world where one thing can also be another."[12] It is a betwixt-and-between state that allows access to the unconscious and mediates between internal opposites, lessening the power of dualistic categories (like gender divisions) and opening up the possibilities in any situation. Women may have a particular tolerance for this mutability, given their more malleable ego boundaries

The trickster's inspiration comes from the profound mutability of the internal imaginal world. In dreams a woman may act in ways unthinkable in waking life. In imagination, women can picture themselves in freer form. The dream, the imaginative picture, is a first step toward the authentic self, an inspiration that may help motivate a woman to challenge the constraints of her own and others' assumptions about her life and its meaning. The inner life of the imagination provides the freedom to reflect, rather than simply react. This is an important resource in any woman's attempt to deconstruct, in her own life, the bond between feminine shadow and masculine shadow.

The conflagration of the wizard and his cronies symbolizes the outburst of energy the accompanies the deconstruction of the bond with the masculine shadow. This fire, taking place at a forestalled wedding, inevitably reminds us of Medea's fiery revenge on Jason's wedding party. And the wings of Fitcher's bird are reminiscent of the wings on which Medea escapes Corinth. The trickster is very good at destroying inauthentic ego adaptations, very good at taking flight, back to a path of her own. But thinking back to Medea's story, we have to wonder, what happens after the conflagration and the dramatic escape?

Women who are confined in inauthentic roles need to preserve some part of the self, to try to keep some aspect of inner life uncontaminated by intrusive role expectations. The more extreme the external constraints are on true individuation, the more women are forced to use covert tactics to preserve that inner self. A woman like Diana, Princess of Wales, who has married into a situation in which her role—as royal figurehead, as producer of heirs—controls her life, is more likely to develop secretive relationships, in an effort to have some place to be authentic. The trickster stance, a stance which justifies cunning, allows a woman just enough internal room to continue to protect the true self but not much room to develop it. The long-term effect of cleverly disguising the true self is that, after a long enough time, that self is no longer known to anyone, the trickster included. This means that dependence on the trickster adaptation eventually disconnects a woman from the inner guidance of the self. As a consequence, women who use the trickster adaptation to escape oppressive circumstances, or who wish they could, often find themselves in new oppressive circumstances that require more tricks.

The trickster adaptation, as a way of life, is a child's solution to the power imbalance that springs from gender inequality. It is an accommodation to patriarchal authority, an authority that is perceived as too overwhelming to stand up to directly. That authority, whether embodied in one's own upbringing and values, in the courts, in popular culture, in one's boss or husband, still, despite our post-feminist condition, dominates the lives of most men and women. This fact can make it seem that any clever way of besting the tyrant (however represented) is admirable. It's easy to become dependent on protective deceptions, to rely on secretiveness to avoid dangerous conflicts, perhaps without really noticing. In a culture that denigrates women's reality, one must to be shrewd about revealing oneself or suffer serious hardship. At the same time, to always be a trickster leads to a loss of authenticity in relationships. So we have a another bind. The trickster adaptation breaks up the union of feminine and masculine shadow and makes some protected, internal room for the feminine self, but it also presents a danger: an habitual inauthenticity that blocks individuation. The trickster is a transitional adaptation, one that should do its protective work, then allow the self to evolve beyond tricksterism. That movement, however, is very often blocked. Fortunately the nature of the self provides opportunities to work through the blocks. Medea's return to Colchis and her immortality are symbolic references to these aspects of the self as we will see below.

The Jungian view of human nature is a profoundly hopeful one, focusing on the unique destiny of each individual. That destiny rests on the persistent nature of the self.[13] The conscious manifestation of the self, at any given point in one's life, may be constrained by circumstance, repressed or contorted by oppressive influences, but it is a resource that cannot be eliminated. It is always available through the unconscious. In this respect, the concept of the self is a concept of radical freedom. This freedom is the journey of the psyche, the journey that is individuation. The self will continue to strive for authenticity, and this is, in part, driving the "trying again and again" pattern. Each repeated episode is an opportunity to come to a new awareness of the nature of the problem, an opportunity to know the self better.

Medea's return to Colchis is a return to her beginning, her roots. This is an appropriate choice for women who find themselves trapped in a repetitive cycle in relationships, whether they are continually overwhelmed by the shadow of intimacy or compulsively use the trickster adaptation to handle that shadow. A woman needs to return to her beginnings in two senses: she needs to understand her upbringing, particularly in terms of her early internalization of the feminine gender role, and she needs to find a home base, a foundation for individuation within herself. That foundation exists in the self.

The reliable basis of the self is symbolized in the Medean myth by Medea's immortality. The closing images of her story, in which she rules an eternal paradise where rebirth is possible, portray archetypal resources within the self and delineates the potential for internal transformation. Throughout her story Medea is portrayed as both divine and mortal, loving and deadly, intent on both hoarding and giving away her magic. She overflows the usual categories, just as the self overflows the ego's categories. Medea in the Elysian Fields is the eternal self, operating in the underworld of the unconscious, overseeing the archetypal potentials of regeneration and rebirth. She is, in this final episode, that aspect of the transpersonal feminine which cannot be destroyed, even if it is driven underground and made mysterious or supposedly unknowable.

As Jung states, we may "define the Self as the totality of the conscious and unconscious psyche, but this totality transcends our vision."[14] The self has ways and means that go beyond the ego's limits. The end of the myth of Medea is an image of this transpersonal aspect of the self, reminding us of its ever-present resources. For guidance as to how to access those resources, we will turn to one more story in our final chapter.

CHAPTER SEVEN

The Real Search:
Finding a Solid Foundation
for the Feminine Self

USING THE MYTH of Medea and two variations of the Bluebeard fairy tale motif, we have explored the shadow of the female gift for facilitating relationships. We have noted the interlinking of that shadow with the masculine shadow, a union which, in aggregate, constitutes the shadow of intimate heterosexual relationships. A number of episodes and images in these stories, most notably the Cauldron of Regeneration, the transformation of the wily sister into Fitcher's "bird," and the reign of Medea in the Elysian Fields, have indicated the transpersonal resources of the feminine self. These resources are tenacious, surviving the confinements of unbalanced, repressive gender roles as well as the wounds of shadow-carrying. But what will enable a woman to return to the home base of the Feminine self, to know and grasp its resources? To understand and clarify that process we will turn to a final fairy tale, one that begins with the familiar Bluebeard figure, only to take a radically different turn.

Elsa and the Evil Wizard

LONG, LONG AGO an evil wizard lived in a beautiful castle high in the mountains. Scattered throughout the garden were statues of young maidens. Sadly, these had once been living girls, snatched from their lives for the wizard's horrible collection.

One morning he decided he needed a statue with long golden hair. He dressed like a fine nobleman, put honey on his lips so that his voice would be sweet, and sprinkled morning dew on his face, giving it a kind expression to mask his natural cruelty. He wrapped himself in his magical flying cloak. It was this cloak which gave him power over maidens: If they stepped on it willingly they were caught. But if they were not willing, it had no power.

The wizard circled and swooped above the valleys until he saw Elsa picking raspberries outside the village, her long beautiful golden hair sparkling in the sun. He floated to the ground, spread his cloak on the path and said, "Beautiful maiden, step on my cloak. Your feet are too dainty and tender for the rough muddy ground."

Elsa laughed, "My feet are quite sturdy, thank you. You should take better care of your cloak."

This had never happened to the wizard before and he was puzzled. He looked around and saw grazing goats. He decided to make them attack Elsa so that he could rescue her and coax her onto the cloak. But when the goats charged Elsa, she ignored his help, escaping by her own efforts. In the confusion, the wizard's cloak got stuck on a goat's horns and ripped. Elsa felt sorry for him then and, using a hawthorn as a needle, sewed up the tear with a strand of her hair.

But the wizard was not in the least grateful. "Come over here and look at how loosely you've stitched this. It will never hold!" Elsa stepped over to see just as he trailed the cloak on the ground and she stepped on it. Instantly the cloak wrapped itself around Elsa and the wizard. As it rose from the ground the wizard's face became evil and he grasped Elsa to him. But the strand of golden hair sewn into the cloak caught on a tree branch and would not let go.

The wizard tugged and tugged but could not free the cloak. Finally, in order to use both hands to pull, he let go of Elsa. She dropped to the path and ran straight home. As soon as she caught her breath, she told her mother all that had happened.

The wizard returned to his castle in the mountains in a rage. After smashing some mirrors and terrifying his servants, he lay down to sleep, but the room was strangely bright. At first he thought the moon was shining in the window, but he soon saw that the golden hair in his cloak was shining bright. He tried to cover the stitches up, but they shone through everything. He hid the cloak in the basement, but the bright light filled the castle. He could not sleep.

The next night the evil wizard tried to cut the golden stitches but no knife could part them. He sliced the mended part right out of the cloak and threw it out the window. But it came right back and he knew he did not have the power to get rid of it. The brilliant light kept him from sleep night after night. He was exhausted. Finally, he could stand it no longer and, taking the cloak, flew down to Elsa's village. Rapping on her window to get her attention, he said, "Open up and talk to me. I won't hurt you."

"I will not talk to you," Elsa said. "Go away."

"I can't sleep!" he cried. "Take your silly hair out of my cloak, or I'll make you suffer." But Elsa's mother had told her the village stories of the wizard, and she knew that, if she did not step on his cloak, he had no power over her. When he saw this, he offered her a sack of gold if only she would take out the thread of hair.

"I don't want your gold," Elsa said.

"I'll give you a farm."

"I don't want your farm!" Elsa did not trust the wizard and nothing would make her let him in. He returned to his castle in a very bad temper, thinking, "This stubborn, silly girl is not afraid of me. How can I demonstrate my power?"

He decided to bring one of his statues back to life in order to impress Elsa. The maiden he released ran home. That night the brilliant light was a little dimmed and the wizard slept some. But the next night it was back as bright as ever. He flew to Elsa's window in a rage, storming and threatening her if she did not remove the stitching.

"I think that seam does very well where it is," Elsa said.

The wizard flew back to his mountain, and he soon realized that he could only sleep if he released a maiden-statue. So, one at a time, he brought the statues back to life, until the maidens were all restored to their families. The golden stitches faded to a mild glow, not enough to keep the wizard awake but enough to let him know that he could not go back to his old ways.[1]

I once read this Scandinavian fairy tale to a friend of mine. Each time Elsa turned the wizard down my friend said, in an admiring tone, "What a sensible girl!" And, of course, Elsa is eminently sensible. However, being sensible is not particularly admired in our culture. In women it has a particular implication—just think of the image of a woman wearing "sensible shoes." Being sensible is being unexciting and unattractive; it is a synonym for "repressed" and "constricted." However Elsa's sensible behavior does not spring from being repressed, inhibited, or timid. It seems to spring from a number of other sources.

When the evil wizard first encounters Elsa, he tries what are apparently his usual methods. He flatters her, saying, "Beautiful maiden, step on my cloak. Your feet are too dainty and tender for the rough muddy ground." This kind of flattery seems designed to appeal to the mystique of femininity, to the idea that women are so very special and delicate that they should not have to deal with the ordinary realities of the outside world. It is an infantilization, an appeal to identificatory love (as described in chapter four) at a very primitive, "you-need-a-daddy-and-I'll-be-one-for-you" level. If a woman is hungry for recognition, she might feel very drawn to the chance to be deemed so special. If she has not had a chance to develop her own ability to deal with the world, the opportunity to be intimate with someone who promises to take care of that for her might be enticing.

Elsa's reply—"My feet are quite sturdy, thank you. You should take better care of your cloak"—amuses us because of the stark contrast between the wizard's flowery attempt at seduction and her down-to-earth response. What makes her so impervious to the wizard's offer to make her special? First, she knows herself; she knows that she is capable. She knows that her feet are sturdy, that she is grounded, that she can handle her environment. She does not need a spurious, trumped-up specialness, because she has a clear view of her real qualities. Second, Elsa has no problem speaking up. The anxious "I-don't-know" syndrome documented by Gilligan in her research has not shut Elsa up.[2] Confronted with male authority, as well as wealth, good looks, and an apparently considerable class difference, Elsa feels no compunction about saying no or about stating her own view of things. She is not afraid to differ; she seems confident of her right to have an opinion.

When the wizard decides to make the grazing goats attack Elsa so that he can rescue and then entrap her, he is making another, more elaborate attempt at infantilizing her. His expectation is, once again, that she is incapable of handling her environment and will bond with someone who is more competent. Elsa ignores his help, escaping by her own efforts. Once again, she knows that she is capable—and she does not feel obliged to bolster a stranger's ego by accepting help she does not need. The notion that women are inherently less able to grapple with the challenges of life is deeply ingrained in our images of femininity. Because of this, some women feel the need to appear less capable, less intelligent, or less assertive than they really are in order to seem feminine and appealing, especially in courtship or potential courtship situations. Elsa obviously feels no such need to mask her competence. At no point does she seem to be seeking approval; she is simply herself. Does the fairy tale give us any clue as to how Elsa developed such a firm foundation within herself?

THE GOOD MOTHER

The story gives us some indication of the source of Elsa's sturdiness. After her initial encounter with the wizard, she "ran straight home. As soon as she caught her breath, she told her mother all that had happened." A bit later we find that, "Elsa's mother had told her the village stories of the wizard, and she knew that, if she did not step on his cloak, he had no power over her." Elsa has a mother who can handle the truth—Elsa feels free to tell her all that has happened. Elsa is, as far as we can tell, not afraid of being criticized by her mother or of overwhelming her mother. She will be heard. And, indeed, Elsa's mother comes through with a very appropriate response: She educates her daughter as to the real nature of the new danger she has encountered.

When girls first start to encounter complex and potentially dangerous situations in relationships, they are often unable to tell their mothers "all that had happened." Many of my psychotherapy clients tell me that their mothers responded to their attempts to confide in and seek guidance from them with criticism, especially if the daughter was describing a scary or disturbing incident. These mothers focused on their daughter's behavior, talking as if nothing difficult would ever happen to a girl as long as she made no mistakes. Thus they steered their daughters away from figuring out how to be safe and toward trying to be perfect. Other clients tell of mothers who were so easily overwhelmed that it seemed hurtful to tell them the truth and expect help. These were mothers who had never developed their own ability to deal with the real world and so could not help their daughters to do so. Still other women became so accustomed to being ignored by their parents that, by the time they began to have encounters with boys and men, they had given up trying to confide in adults. Sometimes this chronic dismissal of the child's attempt to describe her experiences was a general "children-should-be-seen-and-not-heard" injunction, but in other families (as in many American classrooms) it was only the girls who were discouraged from talking about themselves.

In Bianca's opinion, the lack of a competent, attentive mother leads many women to cling to intimacy with a sense of anxiety. I asked her if she had any thoughts about the cause of that anxiety and she replied, "Could it be that we're afraid that if we stop obsessing about relationships, we will exclude men, leave them behind? But I don't think that's it. I think we are not so much afraid of men as we are of other women. I've seen women use their acumen to undermine other women and girls. I've known some mothers who have really dispirited their daughters, inadvertently or not. I think this causes more destruction than men cause, because women can get to the core, strike with more accuracy. I think mothers condition daughters to feel anxiety about striking out on their own path by responding in an undermining way."

Bianca seems to be describing an extreme situation, in

which a mother may be motivated by envy or fear. However, Alice Miller, in her influential book *The Drama of the Gifted Child,* states that adult women commonly, albeit unconsciously, "pass on . . . the contempt they once suffered" as girl children.[3] A mother caught in the grip of this dynamic will feel envy if she sees that her daughter has the freedom to develop that she herself did not have. She will feel contempt when her daughter shows weakness, a reaction that is actually a form of self-disdain. The way in which the mother's individuation was, and is, undermined prevents her from providing a good foundation for her daughter's individuation.

In addition, a mother may feel an unconscious fear when she thinks that her daughter is flaunting convention by striking out on her own path. The mother may act as a socializing agent, because of her sense that an unconventional woman places herself in a dangerous position. If a mother has been taught that a woman will be safe only if she plays the appropriate feminine role, then, in an effort to protect her daughter, she will suppress her daughter's efforts to individuate. It may sound here like I am indulging in a time-honored psychological game called "Put It All On Mom." Yet as long as women have the sole or primary responsibility for childrearing, mothers will be the primary source of guidance in early individuation. Therefore they will also be the primary foundation of the adult woman's internalized attitude toward herself.

Elsa apparently has a mother in whom she can safely confide, who shares in Elsa's concerns. As a result, Elsa has the opportunity to develop her own view of things, her own capacity to consider events. Also, Elsa's mother gives her appropriate guidance, by telling her what is known of the wizard. She does not panic, minimize, or assign blame in response to her daughter's troublesome experience. She takes Elsa's experience seriously, but is not critical or overwhelmed. This provides a good mirroring response for her daughter, a response that accurately mirrors or reflects what is important to Elsa about her own experience. The mother's response allows Elsa to develop a steady image of herself and the world by internalizing her mother's attitude. As Elsa's mother gives her guidance, she assumes that, with her help and information, Elsa will be able to grapple with things. And she is right. Elsa apparently has reason to trust her mother's information, which gives us the sense that her mother has been a reliable source of guidance in the past. Elsa has not experienced her mother as incompetent. Her mother is apparently capable of grappling with her environment and teaches her daughter to do the same, with appropriate help.

If a girl has a mother who can be safely confided in and who can give guidance to her daughter, she can probably avoid repeating destructive patterns in her quest for intimacy. The daughter will not become a woman who assumes that she must have intimacy at any cost, regardless of compatibility or safety. Through her early and consistent experience she will learn, when presented with a difficult relationship situation, to consult her own view of things and to consult trustworthy others rather than depending on her partner's view or on an idealized vision of a perfect relationship. Gilligan found in her study that the adolescent girls who managed to retain some faith in their own view of things were the girls who had truthful, forthright (even if argumentative) conversations with their mothers.[4] Most important, in my opinion, is that, having experienced a wholesome, intimate relationship with her mother in which she can express her authentic self, a girl will know what such a relationship feels like. As a consequence, she will be better equipped to avoid being fooled by an insincere or exploitive seduction and to avoid becoming deeply attached to an impossible partner.

Well, this is great news for those lucky girls and women who have or had such a mother. But what about the rest of us? I believe that one must experience such a relationship in order to internalize and develop the necessary foundation for the feminine self. I also believe that such a relationship can happen at any age and certainly does not have to occur with one's own mother. Lauren has no children, but she does have strong relationships with her nieces. She felt that, at fifty, she had reached a point in life that made it more possible to include assessment in her intimate relationships. In her childhood experiences with her mother, she had primarily learned to tolerate emotional pain, to associate willingness to suffer with intimacy. Having worked her way out of that destructive association, Lauren turned toward the younger women of her family, to try to pass on what she had learned.

"I began," Lauren said, "to talk about all of this with my nieces, who were in their early twenties. I talked to them about whom they were involved with. I said, 'Let's think about this, let's think about the kinds of things that might happen.'" It's important to notice that Lauren did not approach her nieces with a list of rules or an opinionated formulation for how they should act as women or for what constitutes good relationships. This would simply be another way of telling them that they are incapable of developing their own view and assessment of things. Lauren goes on, "We were never taught to develop our own assessments of men's characters. It wasn't in our consciousness and I want it to be in theirs. Maybe if I talk with them, it will be a part of their process to ask, 'Does this relationship work? Does this make sense?'"

If Lauren's nieces have not had the opportunity to internalize this process with their own mothers, they now have an opportunity with Lauren. Women can have such an opportunity with relatives, teachers, friends, in mentor relationships, in women's groups, and in psychotherapy. In Charlotte Brontë's novel *Jane Eyre,* Jane is an orphaned girl whose guardian, an aunt, does not provide her with any mirroring or recognition.[5] On the contrary, her aunt alternately ignores and vilifies her. Eventually Jane is sent to a boarding school where, at first, everyone seems to be like her aunt. But she finds both a teacher and a close friend who listen to her, who want to know who she is and who encourage her to find out what kind of life she wants to live. Jane is, in later life, tempted by a number of inappropriate intimate relationships and rejects them, relying on her own judgment. The crucial factor in reparative relationships, such as the ones Jane Eyre had at school, is that these are relationships in which it is possible for a girl or woman to talk over her experiences and relationships with a trustworthy woman who is interested, experienced, and steady in her regard for them. If the woman (or women) acting as a "mother substitute" is competent, genuinely interested in the girl's welfare, able to listen, able to think with rather than dictate to, then the girl's inner foundation that is necessary for the individuation of the feminine self begins to solidify. When I use the phrase mother substitute, I do not intend to conjure a sentimental picture of caretaking. The necessary relationship is one that encourages self-exploration and the development of good judgment. Such relationships can, over time, be internalized as an aspect of internal reflective space.

It is not necessary that a reparative relationship provide answers or rules for living. The vital activity in such a relationship is the process of finding, elaborating, and validating perceptions, insight, opinions, and feelings, just as we saw Elsa's mother do. When trusted others notice one's responses in an accepting way and when they are not bowled over by those feelings, this can, over time, be taken in to build up the accepting attitude necessary for internal reflection. Mirroring (i.e., accurate feedback from others) and recognition (i.e., acknowledgment and appreciation of one's attributes from others) can be internalized as productive forms of self-reflection. This eventually enables a woman to "know what she knows"; it can undo the undermining "I don't know" that girls learn as adolescence approaches.

EDITING PERFECTION

When the wizard's cloak is ripped, Elsa, feeling sorry for him, sews the tear with a strand of her hair. The wizard uses her good deed to lure her onto the entrapping cloak. Instantly the cloak wraps itself around Elsa and the wizard. As it rises from the ground, the wizard's face reveals his true intentions. But the strand of golden hair sewn into the cloak catches on a tree branch and prevents the wizard from kidnapping Elsa. As in "Fitcher's Bird," the wizard is able to entrap his prey by inspiring pity, by needing help. His cloak catches her, but the golden hair saves her. What does this symbolize?

The cloak's power to stun a woman who steps on it represents a paralysis of will. This paralysis occurs when a woman buys into an image of perfection in relationships. When women edit themselves in an effort to embody that image, withholding and ignoring any responses in themselves that do not fit their picture of a good woman, they begin to lose their inner guidance. Ignoring the self and its communications of feeling, preference, reaction, and perception, seems necessary to maintaining relationships. This was what Cora described as "denying the belly." She remembers, "I would get signs from my gut about what was wrong, but I dismissed them before I even understood them, let alone acted on them." She had learned, as Gilligan puts it, "not to speak about—and eventually not to know—her thoughts and feelings."[6] Focusing on being lovable, on being seen as "nice," makes it difficult for a woman to really hear her gut, and that inner deafness makes it impossible for a woman to know when to act.

I recently read a vivid example of this in a "Dear Abby" advice column. A woman, after describing a completely exploitive and wretched relationship that had been going on for years, ended her letter to Abby with this question: "Please tell me how to get on with my life-sans Rick [her boyfriend] without hurting his feelings."[7] She can act for herself only if she can be assured that she will still be nice. Of course, there is no way to end a relationship without hurting feelings. Fortunately Abby gave the letter writer permission to not be nice, and perhaps, given the blessing of this authority figure, the letter writer was able to do what she knew she wanted and needed to do. Her ability to act was effectively paralyzed by a fear of being less than benevolent.

It is worthwhile at this point to repeat Gilligan's key conclusion concerning this phenomenon of being afraid to appear anything but nice: "As the phrase 'I don't know' enters our interviews with girls at this developmental juncture, we observe girls struggling over speaking and not speaking, knowing and not knowing, feeling and not feeling, and we see the makings of an inner division. We saw this struggle affect their feelings about themselves, their relationships with others, and their ability to act in the world."[8] This inner division constitutes a disconnection from the self that leaves no internal ground for the development of discernment and good judgment. Consequently, women "are in danger of losing their ability to distinguish what is true from what is said to be true, what feels loving from what is said to be love, what feels real from what is said to be reality," as Gilligan says of the girls in her study.[9] This is the effect of the wizard's cloak.

In this state of confusion, a woman is very likely to project her sense of agency, effectiveness, and most important, discernment, onto a man. The ability to assess reality is shifted from a part of the self, or a potential within the self, to an external relationship. Someone outside the self, like Dear Abby in the example above, is given the power to judge. Most often the outside authority is projected onto the partner or onto an ideal image of how a relationship should be. Women who are caught in this projection habitually put aside what they notice, what they know on a gut level, and accept in place of this knowledge a received opinion, a construct about the relationship they are living. The power to delineate reality, to decide what is important, is handed over to the partner, to the ideal vision of the relationship, or to both.

The golden hair that Elsa used to help the wizard saves her after she steps on the cloak. Her ready empathy seems to have gotten her into trouble, as did the empathy of the unsuspecting women in "Fitcher's Bird," but the product of that empathy, the stitches in the cloak, also saves her. The thread catches the cloak after the wizard's true nature has been revealed. I think that the order of events here is important. Anyone with normal compassion for others can be fooled once by an unscrupulous person who appears to need help. What we have been trying to understand in all of our discussion is why some women can be taken in, through their sense of empathy, by the same unscrupulous person multiple times. Elsa can be taken in only once, and the line of golden stitches symbolizes her ability to learn from that bad experience. She does not try to talk herself out of what she has seen on the wizard's face. She does not feel that his behavior is her responsibility. She does not want to save him from his own nature. The golden stitches represent her willingness to "know what she knows" and to act on it. The golden seam catches her mistake, preventing it from destroying her life. The full nature of the golden hair is revealed when the wizard goes home.

When the wizard tries to sleep he finds that his room is strangely bright. It's not the moon shining in the window, but the golden hair in his cloak shining brightly. He tries to cover up the stitches but they glow through everything. He hides the cloak in the basement, but the bright light fills the castle. He cannot sleep. The golden hair is the light of insight, a spark of self-knowledge. Elsa's ability to reflect on her experience, to consider it, and to seek help in understanding her experience halts the wizard's repetitive shadow relationships. Until Elsa, all confrontations between the wizard and various women have ended in a frozen loss of consciousness. Now the light of consciousness has entered this destructive pattern.

CHANGING DESTRUCTIVE PATTERNS

So far I have approached the characters in this fairy tale as examples of the masculine shadow of intimacy (in the case of the wizard) and of a well-founded feminine self able to resist acting out the feminine shadow of intimacy (Elsa). Now I want to shift perspectives and address the tale as a paradigm for relationships between parts of the self. Looking at the *dramatis personae* of the story in this way, we can see the wizard with his paralyzing cloak and his driven behavior as the personification of a repetition compulsion, a pattern of relationships in which the same conflict is unconsciously recreated with each new partner, or which is acted out as a recurrent pattern within the same relationship. The wizard is an unconscious complex, a set of emotions, beliefs, memories and attitudes of which the conscious mind is unaware, that powers the repetition compulsion. In the circumstance of courtship and intimacy, the complex takes over the ego, freezing its ability to learn, choose, and consider. Such an unconscious complex is, in its outer layers, full of personal memories, feelings, and beliefs. These outer layers are the beliefs, self-representations, emotions, and judgments that we have been discussing, the baggage carried in the quest for intimacy, in an individualized form determined by the woman's particular personal experiences. The way in which such complexes function means that mere intellectual acknowledgment of the repetition compulsion does not stop it. This is why a woman can be very smart like Hannah Arendt, very powerful like Medea, very accomplished like Claire Bloom (all attributes shared by Cora, Lauren, and Bianca) and still act out a destructive pattern in relationships.

What will stop a repetitive, harmful relationship pattern, if intellectual insight won't? First, a woman must be willing to see, to look relentlessly, just as the glowing golden stitches force the wizard to keep his eyes open. This is painful and requires support. Support groups and/or psychotherapy are important, perhaps indispensable to halting a repetition compulsion. Because of the paralyzing quality of the complex, other people are more likely to notice its onset than the person experiencing it. Talking regularly to a person (or persons) who know her well enough to say, "Wait a minute, this sounds familiar," is a necessary first phase in a woman's struggle with destructive relationships. The repetition compulsion functions like the wizard's cloak, freezing the woman's ability to act on what she knows. She becomes mired in her own version of the fantasy contract we discussed in chapter four. The perceptions of a good support group or psychotherapist act like the golden thread in the cloak; they put a hitch into the momentum of the repetition compulsion.

Relationships in support groups and therapy like this can

provide the needed substitute mother. Over a period of time, a woman begins to internalize the reflections that the therapist or group members offer concerning her pattern in relationships. It is not so much the specific opinions or perspectives of these supportive others that need to be internalized but the ability to reflect on the repetitive pattern when the compulsion is activated. This happens through the process of telling trusted, perceptive, honest others about destructive relationships when those relationships are starting and while they are going on, and being willing to listen to their view of what is going on. It's important that everyone involved in such an endeavor, both the woman telling her tale and those listening, know that this may need to be discussed many times. Sometimes the insights involved are extremely simple, as when Cora realized, "What I learned is, I don't have to suffer like this. It was a revelation, that I could choose not to suffer." I cannot emphasize enough that this is not a process of achieving intellectual insight. If it were, one conversation would be enough. It is a process of developing the ability to look at, see clearly, and reflect on the parts of the self that are activated by intimacy or its prospect, and to develop a more conscious relationship toward those aspects. The shift in attitude toward the self must sink in emotionally. This is analogous to developing "muscle memory" in sports training, the phenomenon in which, after sufficient time and practice, a physical activity can be done without being thought about.

Over the course of long-term, reliable, reflective relationships with other women, or one other woman, the ability to reflect builds up what can best be described as an internal space. One begins to have the mental room to consider reality, both personal and interpersonal. The compulsion is no longer in control of behavior. An internal reflective space allows internal and external life to be observed and allows formerly intolerable feelings to be tolerated. The support of a therapist and/or group is also vital to the ability to tolerate difficult feelings. Anxiety, desperation, emptiness, and self-loathing are all, as we have seen, part of the shadow of a woman's quest for intimacy. A woman who lacked a competent, trustworthy, comforting mother in childhood and adolescence not only is unable to sufficiently comfort herself, but also lacks inner steadiness in the face of distress. Trustworthy relationships in adulthood begin to model what is lacking, allowing it to slowly be built up as a part of the self.

The evil wizard tries to cut the golden stitches of Elsa's hair, but they cannot be cut. Even when he slices the mended part right out of the cloak and throws it away, it comes back. He does not have the power to get rid of it. The brilliant light of the golden seam keeps him from sleep night after night. It is necessary to stay awake—that is, to stay aware or conscious—if one is to end the repetition of destructive patterns. Fortunately, once insight has invaded a repetition compulsion in a genuine, effective way, it is nearly impossible to entirely put out the light of that insight. A genuine insight involves thought and feeling, mind and body coming together in an experience of understanding that is more than cognitive. It is what I would call a full-body insight. It has impact. For me a useful, productive insight incorporates movement, by which I mean that the full-body insight produces further understanding, induces a potent shift in one's relationship to oneself and/or to the material being explored. It moves; it leads into something. Such an insight causes a significant change in mood, feeling, belief, or behavior. It is not the end of understanding (not an experience of "that's that") but the expansive beginning of exploration.

If that movement and exploration is allowed, and given support through good relationships, then individuation will begin to guide psychological life. This guidance is a process in which reactions, feelings, perceptions, and intuitions that well up from within, from the unconscious, are taken seriously by the ego and used to steer both external choices and internal exploration. For instance, if Cora had been guided by her feelings and psychosomatic symptoms during her relationship, rather than her "ideal vision," those reactions would have taken her in a much more authentic direction. As a person develops more ability to reflect on the spontaneous reactions that come up from the unconscious, more unconscious material is brought to consciousness. Individuation is a normal process that will simply proceed if it is not blocked by some unresolved conflict within the self. The repetition compulsion displayed in destructive relationship patterns is just such a conflict. The acting out of the pattern impedes the ability to reflect on the inner guidance that steers normal individuation. How does a woman begin to say no to the compulsive behavior?

SAYING NO

Finally, exhausted from lack of sleep, the wizard flies down to Elsa's window and tries to talk with her. She refuses to open her window and talk to him. He threatens her but, armed with the necessary information from her mother, she is not intimidated. The wizard tries to bribe her into removing the gold stitches, but to no avail. Elsa now knows that she cannot trust the wizard and nothing will convince her otherwise. She continues to say no.

It is notoriously difficult for women to say no. Women who say no are frequently seen as bitches, witches, prudes: they are too sensible, too serious, too negative, too timid. Since women generally fear the prospect of being unlovable, unpleasant, or imperfect, they make every effort to avoid being labeled bitch, witch, or prude. For women, compliance—saying yes—is often confused with receptivity, insufficient self-protection is confused with graciousness, and lack of necessary boundaries is confused with being accepting or loving. Many psychologists have attributed these problems to the gender differences in early childhood development that we have already discussed, differences that result in women's talent for and emphasis on relationships.[10] As you might anticipate, I do not agree with this assessment. When a woman has striven since adolescence to embody an idealized image of womanhood, she does so at the expense of knowing the self. She is disconnected from the self, or at least from those parts of the self that do not fit the idealized gender role. When Gilligan observes "the makings of an inner division" in pubescent girls, she sees the nascent disconnection of an ego that is struggling to be perfect, nice, and lovable from the authentic self, which includes many parts that do not appear perfect. When women habitually put aside what they notice, what they know on a gut level, the result is an embedded, habitual disconnection in the way ego relates to self.

The ego in this situation has difficulty acknowledging

and validating gut-level perception and shows a tendency towards perfectionism. Perfectionism is incorporated in consciousness as a set of abstract, disembodied rules about how a woman is supposed to be. These rules act as a particularly thick and constraining filter, screening out all emotional, somatic, and symbolic communications from the self that might deter the ego from identifying with a particular role. Spontaneous responses, especially responses of "no," are deeply distrusted. This begins to blot out the normal, self-protective "no" response to intrusion, disrespect, and danger. Instead, a rigid "no" response develops in relation to any situation that might lead to conflict. This eventually becomes almost automatic, effectively cutting off the self's line of communication to the ego. So, when Cora began to experience gut-level doubts about her relationship and to suffer psychosomatic symptoms, she was receiving inner guidance from the self. However, she was allowing herself to be guided instead by her ideal vision of what the relationship should or could be.

Reclamation of the inner guidance that allows us to say "no" when required does simply result from cognitive analysis. The emotions and body are crucial to this reclamation process. The emotions and the body constantly communicate important perceptions about people and situations. Being intruded on, being treated with disrespect, being threatened, produce certain visceral reactions. Each person must develop her own awareness of these reactions. I find that many spontaneous emotional and somatic responses are so automatically dismissed that they are not even noticed by the person having them. For this reason, although Cora perceives her feelings and symptoms as important in retrospect, at the time she saw them as a sign of personal weakness, not as signs of something amiss in the relationship. It's important to consider every noticeable response. If a reaction proves to be fruitless, fine, disregard it. Essentially a woman needs to build up her own ability to assess of the accuracy of all her feelings, intuition, perceptions, and somatic or gut responses rather than to deal only with those inner communications that make it through the ego-filter, that filter having been constructed by familial and cultural influences and injunctions. This is a process of trying to actually know what you know, rather than to habitually dismiss what you know before it can be understood.

It is necessary in this process to listen for the tone of one's own inner voice. When undertaking the reclamation of inner guidance, one essentially talks to oneself a great deal. One's tone of voice is powerful; it sets the atmosphere for self-observation as surely as external tone of voice determines the atmosphere of a conversation between two people. In listening to others talk about themselves we notice their tone—the friend whose every minor misstep brings on a flood of vicious self criticism, the co-worker who blandly minimizes even the most obvious emotions, the relative who is always confused about her own opinion. In listening to others, it's relatively easy to notice how this habitual tone affects the way the person understands herself. In the same way, the tone of the inner voice impacts the way in which you understand yourself, the way in which you understand inner guidance.

The wizard brings one of his maiden-statues back to life in order to impress Elsa. The maiden he releases runs home and that night the brilliant light of the golden stitches dims so that the wizard can sleep some. But the next night it comes back as bright as ever. He flies to Elsa's window in a rage, threatening her if she does not remove the stitching. Elsa, as before, is impervious to his threats. The wizard soon realizes that he can sleep only if he releases a maiden-statue. So, one at a time, he brings the statues back to life, until all the maidens are restored to their families. At this point the golden stitches fade to a mild glow, not enough to keep the wizard awake but enough to let him know that he cannot go back to his old ways.

This final episode of the fairy tale shows us what becomes possible after a repetition compulsion stops. It becomes possible to explore the unconscious, to bring to life both the repressed parts of the self that have been pushed aside, and to activate potentials in the self that have never been known. The captured maidens are petrified, depicting the parts of the self that have been frozen out of conscious life. When a woman is caught in a pattern of destructive relationships, when the compulsion symbolized by the wizard and his cloak runs a woman's relational life, she has no internal room in which to reflect on undeveloped parts of the self. The compulsive behavior and constant drama of these relationships leaves little energy for self-exploration. The fantasy contract is in force, and the woman believes that the intimate relationship, and only that, will fulfill her destiny. Many aspects of the self, here symbolized by the maidens, are frozen out of consciousness, some because they do not fit the woman's image of proper femininity and others because the time, attention, and energy they require to develop is simply not available.

Jung's conceptualization of the unconscious provides us with a way of understanding the psychological, emotional, and spiritual experience portrayed by the statues and their reanimation. For most women, this means the ego is concerned with being a lovable, nice woman. This conscious concern needs to be balanced or compensated by guidance from the unconscious.[11] The compensatory purpose of the unconscious is to balance and regenerate consciousness by communicating denied aspects of the self to the ego. Thus the unconscious functions as a storehouse of forgotten resources. These resources, in this fairy tale, are embodied in the statues.

How are these unconscious resources accessed? First the ego must change. Elsa represents the appropriate ego stance, one that will allow the benumbed parts of the self to breathe again. Her behavior illustrates the results of necessary, conscious work on the ego—work such as learning to trust one's own perceptions, to value oneself, to say no when necessary, and to find relationships which will mirror and nourish one's true self. In the course of that work, the resources of the unconscious can begin to effectively balance conscious development. The unconscious communicates through dreams, emotions, fantasies, projections, and bodily feelings. The ego has become strong enough to be a partner in this intense work of individuation and, as a consequence, can begin to listen to these communications from within. This is another way of saying that individuation, the manifestation of the authentic self over time, can begin to guide life through dialogue between the ego and the unconscious.

The vocabulary of this dialogue between the ego and the unconscious is symbolic. Spontaneous images and narratives encountered in dreams, trance states (however induced), and states of reverie such as daydreams are clues that may lead to an experience of the self. Communications from the unconscious are woven throughout the warp of everyday life. The products of the imagination are continuous and available to all. The real difficulty lies in noticing and validating the daily communications of the unconscious. People habitually ignore, having been trained to do so, the passing thoughts, feelings, images, and body sensations that are the vocabulary of unconscious parts of the self. Once again, Cora's tendency to ignore her gut reactions comes to mind as an example. The ego must retrain and develop the willingness to attend to these communications. Once again, this retraining most effectively takes place through reparative relationships, relationships with others who attend to the communications of the unconscious, who are interested in the true self.

When a woman begins working on the issues involved in a destructive relationship pattern, she will encounter more of the unconscious. Elsa, the ego figure in our story, struggles with the wizard, who characterizes a complex that engenders a repetition compulsion. She brings the necessary ego skills and capacities to bear on the struggle with the wizard. As a seeming byproduct of the encounter between Elsa and the wizard, the statues are reanimated. This, I think, illustrates both the structure and processes of the psyche. Working on personal problems leads to deeper experience because the unconscious is both personal and transpersonal. The personal unconscious consists of repressed memories, feelings, preferences, and capacities. This repressed material springs from the individual experiences of life with which, for a variety of reasons, the ego will not or cannot form a conscious, workable relationship. A complex is, in its outer layers, full of personal memories, feelings, and beliefs; the ego must come to terms with these layers in order to deconstruct the complex and be free of its paralyzing grip. These outer layers are the beliefs, self-representations, emotions, and judgments that we have been discussing, the baggage carried by the quest for intimacy; they are the fantasy contract in action.

The statue-maidens represent these complexes. They are forever stuck in place in the unconscious unless and until the ego develops the ability to reflect upon them. The maiden-statues represent the way in which a life devoid of self-reflection leads to a living death, stuckness, a loss of connection and growth. The image of the statues frozen in stone forcefully illustrates how necessary an internal reflective space is in the process of transformation. Viewing the statues and Elsa as parts of the psyche, Elsa being the conscious ego and the statues being unconscious complexes, the fairy tale's ending makes it clear that even a major transformative experience is not the end of individuation. Learning to trust one's own perceptions, to value oneself, to say no when necessary, to find relationships that will mirror and nourish one's true self, are not an end but a beginning, the beginning of bringing the unconscious aspects of the self to life.

Individuation has no end. Some aspects of the psyche are always waiting to be explored, to melt in the light of consciousness, and to participate in life. When the ego is able to relate to the authentic self and attend to the self's communications through dialogue with the unconscious, then individuation, the discovery and integration of the authentic self, is furthered. Individuation inevitably involves dualities; opposites emerge within as the self becomes more fully known. The undeveloped parts of the self are oftentimes in conflict, seemingly opposed to the conscious ego, just as Cora's feelings about her relationship tended to be opposed to her conscious ideas about the relationship. Becoming conscious of and resolving these internal opposites is the daily work of individuation. For women, this process of resolving internal opposites is complicated by the way in which the dualities of our culture are projected onto gender roles.

HAVING MY OWN LIFE

The coming together of polar opposites within the self is symbolically imagined as a sacred marriage, something that Jung called a *coniunctio* (Latin, "union").[12] The sacred marriage is both a sign of and a prelude to the experience of wholeness. It is an expansion of consciousness. Robert Hopcke, a Jungian theorist and psychotherapist, sees the coniunctio as "a guiding image and evocative challenge to each individual concerned with inner resolution and outer relatedness."[13] The female quest for intimacy is a search for coniunctio. However, social conditioning and the psychological process of projection lead heterosexual women to vest the ability to fully realize the self in the image of a male partner. Consequently, the heterosexual woman seeks inner resolution by trying to make the external marriage (i.e., relationship) sacred. And she is mightily encouraged in this through the narratives she lives in and by. From the ballads of ancient chivalric tradition to the story line of rock songs, in popular movies, romance novels, and self-help books, the path to wholeness and the path to the right man are presented as the same path.

Earlier we discussed Guggenbühl-Craig's distinction between seeking well-being and seeking salvation in intimacy, salvation being defined as the development of the authentic self through relationships. I concluded that women, in general, seem to be seeking salvation rather than well-being, and that this seeking is, in essence, an archetypally-powered quest. I have reached a further conclusion that, although the development of the authentic self through an intimate partnership is possible, it is highly improbable in heterosexual relationships. Despite this, heterosexual women are continually drawn to attempt this quest with men, for a number of compelling reasons. First, because women's perspectives and experiences continue to be, for the most part, closed out of the mainstream, women are drawn to love their male partners with an identificatory love. Identificatory love is based not on appreciation of the partner as a separate human being, but on identifying with the partner as a representative of the ego ideal, as one who holds the power to give recognition and provide a place in the world. Second, an ideology of love, amounting almost to a religion, continues, in alliance with a still powerful creed of feminine mystique, to give women the message that meaning in life rests on success in an intimate, sexual partnership; the message is not that meaning in life evolves out of all relationships, including one's relationship with one's self, but that it springs primarily, or perhaps only, from the partnership with a man and the family that results from that partnership.

These two factors—identificatory love and the ideology of love—encourage women to endow their intimate relationships with a life-and-death level of meaning, in which the only imaginable route to significant recognition, mirroring, and purpose is through the romantic relationship. The normal, universal questions—"who will love me for myself?" "whose love will help me become myself?"—are amplified and distorted. These questions become the only important questions of a woman's life and the "right" answer to such questions must be a certain kind of man.

Bianca is single right now and her spontaneous, gut-level experience is one of being free and happy. However she is plagued by an internal voice that says, "You'll regret it." Bianca says, "If I'm in a really good space then that voice of fear will be followed by another voice saying, 'No, you've made it.' I feel that I made it to dry land. My sense of myself and my life is solid. Thank goodness. I'm so grateful. My happiness isn't based on whether I'm making the grade in a relationship or at work. It's based on whether I'm good to the people I see everyday and whether they are good to me. Is the sun warm on my skin? Is the rain wet on my jacket? However, it's a lot of work not to let the stereotypes of what I *should* care about take that away with relentless self-questioning. I've worked a lot with couples—I've seen a lot of destruction in those relationships. When I think about that, I think, 'My life is pretty good.' I've made it to dry land and I didn't get shot. I've thought, 'They burned women for this in earlier years.' I just worry that society might revenge itself on me for being too free. That aura of fear contributes to my guilt—I think that I've wanted too much. I sometimes feel guilty that other women are carrying the burden of looking after others and I'm not. I feel like a pioneer. I don't have guidance for living this way." When a woman begins to establish a firm foundation for her feminine self, these are the dilemmas that emerge. Guilt—"I am a selfish and therefore bad woman"—is followed by fear—"bad things happen to bad women."

A final reason that women feel compelled to continue the quest for intimacy, in its asymmetric, perhaps impossible, form, is that, if women don't invest this high level of significance, energy, and importance in intimacy, then intimacy, with all of its practical (in the form of caretaking) and spiritual (in the form of finding meaning in the material world) baggage, will not be maintained. The prospect of this provokes fear, anxiety, and guilt in women. All three women I interviewed spoke of how they had been trained never to abandon loved ones. After the ego work is done, after a solid foundation for individuation is established in a woman's personality, pressure from these feelings of worry and compunction increase rather than decrease. Women seem to ask themselves, as Bianca seems to be asking herself, "Do I have the right to have my own life, even if other women, or my family, or my friends don't have theirs?"

As the normal process of individuation proceeds, women are hit with extraordinary pressures. These spring from the many cultural splits that constitute the collective underpinnings of the search for meaningful relationships. Culture's splitting of autonomy and togetherness, self and relationship, Eros and Logos, culture and nature creates an environment that constantly threatens to derail female individuation. Heterosexual relationships are established across a chasm of cultural differences—the opposing cliffs occupied by denizens of Mars and Venus, according to popular usage—and, since women are generally in charge of maintaining relationships, the strain of staying connected across the chasm falls disproportionately on them. Women are constantly distracted from the process of their own individuation by the impact of our dualistic cultural environment and the baggage that dualism places on the quest for intimacy. (I'm sure that male individuation is also affected by this but in very different ways, ways that will have to be explicated in another book, preferably written by a man.)

It is certainly possible to discard some of the baggage carried by the quest, to disconnect oneself from some of the underpinnings. Carolyn Heilbrun, in her book *The Last Gift of Time*, counsels women to accept that men are not listeners, that they do not change, as women do, and that men do not consider female knowledge to be actual knowledge.[14] Heilbrun is a prolific feminist scholar and literary critic who taught at Columbia for thirty-three years. She considers herself to be happily married but does not expect her husband to understand her. She has divested her personal, intimate partnership of the drive to bring feminine values to bear on the patriarchal mainstream. She does not expect sexual and familial intimacy to help her realize and express her inner reality. She has focused that drive onto her own writings. In our last conversation, I told Cora about Heilbrun's stance. She was both relieved and horrified by the idea. "What a relief that would be, but doesn't it sell men short?" she said.

As I bring this book to a conclusion, I must admit that I

do not know the answer to Cora's question. Does it sell men short? I suppose, ultimately, that men, or each individual man, must answer that question. Women need to become conscious of their own purposes in their quest for intimacy. They need to return to a home base within the self, to develop a firm foundation for the feminine self. From the solid ground of that foundation, a woman can begin to survey and clarify the personal and collective baggage that weighs down her search for a meaningful relationship. She can begin to grasp the contradictory cultural underpinnings of that quest and deal with them consciously rather than being driven by them unconsciously. Only then can the possible relationship become plausible.

I came across a lovely statement made by Jungian analyst Ann Ulanov about the way in which Eros and Logos are presented as dualities, as though emotional meaning is inherently opposed to objective truth. "These dualities are questionable. The way they are posed implies that we reach love through one modality, Eros, and truth through another, Logos, and that, in order to reach the transpersonal, the personal is not elevated but abrogated altogether. In fact love and truth are not so easily separated; they are constantly to be found within each other. What is love is also truth for those who love, and what is truth is also love, and the transpersonal is invariably reached, connected to and made incarnate by precisely the personal demand and desires of love."[15] I believe this wholeheartedly. Truth can be reached in the quest for love, and love can be manifested in the search for truth.

However, such a union of truth and love is by its nature fleeting and cannot be made concrete in a relationship. Nor can truth and love be embodied in our lives by particular people. The important question seems to be, "In a given relationship are such experiences possible—not perpetual, or even predictable, but possible?" Returning to those vital questions, "Who will love me for myself?" and "Whose love will help me to become myself?" we can use them as guides in choosing relationships. But this will work only if the answers to these questions are not predetermined. The person who loves you for yourself is not always your husband; the person or persons whose love will help you become yourself does not have to be the person you are sleeping with. The union of truth and love, within a relationship, may occur in very unexpected ways. This is a possible reality, a union of supposed opposites that we rarely experience. Perhaps we can use this image as a north star, to guide our quest for intimacy.

NOTES

Introduction

a. M. L. von Franz, *Interpretation of Fairytales* (Dallas: Spring Publications, 1970), pp. 1–26.

b. C. G. Jung, *Psychological Reflections* (Princeton, NJ: Princeton University Press, 1974), p. 256.

c. Robert Graves, *The Greek Myths,* vol. 2 (New York: Viking Penguin, 1975). The story of Medea, as told in the introduction and in chapters two through five, is taken from pp. 236–57, except as otherwise noted.

d. Andrew Lang, *The Blue Fairy Book* (Magnolia, MA: Peter Smith, 1989), p. 290–4.

Chapter One

1. Carol Gilligan, *In a Different Voice: Psychological Theory and Women's Development* (Cambridge, MA: Harvard University Press, 1982), p. 171.

2. Deborah Tannen, *You Just Don't Understand* (New York: Ballantine, 1990), p. 25.

3. Betty Friedan, *The Feminine Mystique* (New York: W. W. Norton, 1963), p. 47.

4. See Marilyn French, *The Women's Room* (New York: Ballantine, 1988).

5. Nancy Chodorow, *The Reproduction of Mothering* (Berkeley: University of California Press, 1978), pp. 24–7.

6. Jean Baker Miller, "The Development of Women's Sense of Self," in *Women's Growth in Connection,* ed. Jordan et al. (New York: Guilford Press, 1990), p. 16.

7. Charlene Spretnak, "Ecofeminism: Our Roots and Flowering," in *Reweaving the World,* ed. Irene Diamond and Gloria Feman Orenstein (San Francisco: Sierra Club Books, 1990), p. 13.

8. Julia Russel, "The Evolution of an Ecofeminist," in *Reweaving the World,* ed. Irene Diamond and Gloria Feman Orenstein (San Francisco: Sierra Club Books, 1990), p. 225.

9. Annie Cheathem and Mary Powell, *This Way Daybreak Comes* (Philadelphia: New Society Publishers, 1986), p. xix.

10. Ibid., p. 223.

11. Phyllis Grosskurth, "The New Psychology of Women," *New York Review of Books,* 24 October 1991, p. 27.

Chapter Two

1. Lang, *Fairy Book,* p. 290.

2. Judith Herman, *Trauma and Recovery* (New York: Basic Books, 1992), p. 82.

3. *The Complete Grimms' Fairy Tales* (New York: Pantheon, 1972), pp. 216–19.

4. Lang, *Fairy Book,* p. 292.

5. Yumi Wilson, "Domestic Violence," *San Francisco Chronicle,* 13 February 1997, sec. A, p. 20.

6. Gilligan, *Different Voice,* p. 171.

7. Tannen, *Don't Understand,* p. 25.

8. Alan Ryan, "Dangerous Liaison," *New York Review of Books,* 11 January 1996, p. 23.

9. See Hannah Arendt, *The Origins of Totalitarianism* (New York: Harcourt Brace, 1968) and *Eichmann in Jerusalem* (New York: Viking Penguin, 1994).

10. The story of Arendt and Heidegger is taken from Elsbieta Ettinger, *Hannah Arendt/Martin Heidegger* (New Haven, CT: Yale University Press, 1995), pp. 16–19, 28–33, 36–9, 42–7, 50–1, 56–7, 62–71, 76–9, 84–5, 88–9, 96–7, 100–7, 110–11, 114–17, 124–5, 130–2.

11. Ryan, "Liaison," pp. 22–6.

12. Robert Wistrich, "A Fine Romance," *Commentary* (February 1996): 58–60.

13. Ryan, "Liaison," p. 22.

Chapter Three

1. Graves, *Greek Myths.*

2. Juanita Williams, *Psychology of Women: Behavior in a Biosocial Context* (New York: W. W. Norton, 1987), pp. 377–8.

3. Edwin Schur, *Labeling Women Deviant* (Philadelphia: Temple University Press, 1988), p. 208.

4. Gallop Survey of Most Admired Americans (Princeton, NJ: Gallop News Service, 1997).

5. Jean Baker Miller, *Toward a New Psychology of Women,* 2nd ed. (Boston: Beacon Press, 1986), p. 23.

6. Ibid., p. 88; and Miller, "Sense of Self," p. 12.

7. Bernard Whiltey, "Sex Role Orientation and Self-Esteem," *Journal of Personality and Social Psychology* 44, no. 4 (1983): 765–78.

8. Schur, *Deviant,* p. 209.

9. Arlie Russel Hochschild and Anne Machung, *The Second Shift* (New York: Avon, 1990).

10. Carol Gilligan quoted in Anna Quindlen's "Gal Pals," *San Francisco Examiner Magazine,* March 2, 1997, pp. 15, 24–5.

11. Miller, *Psychology of Women,* p. 23.

12. Nor Hall, *The Moon and the Virgin* (New York: Harper & Row, 1980), pp. 64–5.

13. Friedan, *Feminine Mystique,* p. 42.

14. See Eric Neuman, *Amor and Psyche* (Princeton, NJ: Princeton University Press, 1956). This assumption is a premise of this entire work but is particularly clear in the conclusion, pp. 149–52.

15. Carol Gilligan, *Meeting at the Crossroads* (New York: Ballantine, 1992).

16. One of the first signs of Medea's power is her ability to lull the dragon that guards the fleece. The dragon is a creature whose meaning changes a great deal from culture to culture. In Asia, the dragon may represent the power that underlies reality. In Western stories, the dragon has a more chaotic quality, symbolizing those overpowering aspects of nature that prevent individuals from attaining their goals. Many traditional Jungian theorists have perceived this aspect of nature embodied in the dragon as an aspect of the archetypal feminine.(Neuman, *Amor and Psyche,* p. 132.)

This association of woman and nature is a common one in the Western worldview, in that both woman and nature are experienced as chaotic forces in need of masculine control. (Susan Griffin, *Women and Nature: The Roaring Inside Her* [New York: Harper & Row, 1978.]) The male hero's task is, typically, to kill the dragon, to master the forces of chaos, just as, in personal individuation, the heroic ego masters the shadow. But that does not happen in this myth. Medea does not kill the dragon, she enchants it.

This seems to fit with Medea's role as a priestess of Hecate, a woman at home with the darker aspects of life. She deals with the fierce forces of nature by enchanting them, by befriending them in some way, by making a particular kind of relationship to them. I assume that this can be done only by one who has a fine understanding of the creature she is dealing with, which in this case is the dragon. In this act, Medea puts on the mantle of a very ancient goddess figure, the "Mistress of animals." The mistress of animals is an aspect of the Great Goddess thought by Marija Gimbutas to reach back to Paleolithic times. The mistress of animals does not kill animals, she sways them, through her connection to them. She is not in control of the forces of nature but rather consonant with the forces of nature, moving with them in a cyclical round of decay and regeneration. (Marija Gimbutas, *The Language of the Goddess* [San Francisco: Harper & Row, 1989], 109–11.) She relates to the shadow rather than conquering it. Medea's special access to the Golden Fleece, which gives Jason access, may also signal her association with this aspect of the archetypal feminine.

What does the Golden Fleece symbolize? First, why is it gold? According to the Archives for Research in Archetypal Symbolism, gold is "one of the oldest and most universal of religious symbols." (Beverly Moon, ed. *Archetypal Symbolism* [Boston: Shambala, 1991], 304.) It is resistant to chemical reactions, incorruptible, luminous, and rare. Gold is associated with spirit, immortality, and the possibility of perfection. When an ordinary object, as a fleece was in that time and place, has turned gold, it becomes an alchemical object, symbolizing the possibility of transforming ordinary life into something of high value. In this way, the fleece may embody the possibility of immanent spiritual meaning in everyday life.

The fleece links Medea and Jason back to a form of immanent spiritual experience predating Greek civilization According to Walter Burkert, a historian specializing in ancient Greece, a heroic quest, like Jason's for the fleece, is a version of the shaman's ecstatic journey through worlds beyond the everyday, a form of spiritual quest common in hunting societies.

(W. Burkert, *Structure and History in Greek Mythology and Ritual* [Berkeley: University of California Press, 1980], 88–95.) The shaman's vision quest is a dramatic, focused expression of immanent spirituality. The nature of the journey plays out and portrays the interwoven, interpenetrated relationships of individual, community, spirit, and nature.

The shaman may meet a mistress or master of animals (like Medea) who guides him or her and, may also encounter outlandish, special animals (like the dragon). The shaman is often guided to particular objects in the journey (like the fleece) that serve as talismans and become numinous reminders of the quest experience. Burkert goes on to make the case that certain old Great Goddess cults retained, in story and ritual, a vestige of the shamanic journey, encouraging cult devotees to pursue ecstatic experiences of spiritual reality, to form special relationships to particular animals, and to worship the goddess in a wild, mistress-of-the-animals form. Rituals "involving killing and guilt, bloodshed and sexuality, success and failure, superiority and inferiority, death and life" were primary in these cults. (Burkert, *Greek Mythology and Ritual*, 120.)

Medea's connection to the fleece, a talisman of the animal world, and the way in which her story plays out the themes of "killing and guilt, bloodshed and sexuality, success and failure, superiority and inferiority, death and life" indicates her connection to these ancient cults. What has Medea's connection to archaic goddess worship got to do with understanding the female quest for intimacy? I think that many women are attracted to stories and images that relate to the archaic Great Goddesses because those images and narratives bring muted female culture into a relationship to the larger culture. These narratives reflect a multilayered reality, a less boundaried, more interrelated vision of the world and how it works, a vision that may reflect something important about the inner world of women.

A striking aspect of the archaic Great Goddess tradition is its multifaceted, seemingly paradoxical nature, encompassing traits, abilities, and intentions that cross our categories of good and evil, masculine and feminine. These were goddesses of life, death and regeneration who, according to Marija Gimbutas were "givers of life and wielders of destructive powers . . . encompassing the archetypal unity and multiplicity of feminine nature . . . a feminine nature that, like the moon, is light as well as dark." (Marija Gimbutas, *Gods and Goddesses of Old Europe* [Berkeley: University of California Press, 1982], 52.) The goddess was life giving and life taking, generative and destructive, an embodiment of the principle of Eros. The primordial motif of the destroyer/regenatrix portrays, in female imagery, the linked cosmic forces of destruction and creation. (Gimbutas, *Language,* 209–11.) In this imagery we see both the light and shadow of relationship magic, united in one embodiment.

17. Max Weber, qtd. in Jessica Benjamin, *The Bonds of Love* (New York: Pantheon, 1988), p. 109.

18. Jessica Benjamin, *The Bonds of Love* (New York: Pantheon, 1988), p. 206.

19. Joseph Campbell, *Hero with a Thousand Faces* (Princeton, NJ: Princeton University Press, 1949), pp. 109–20.

20. Chodorow, *Reproduction,* pp. 51–60.

21. Shirley Ardener, ed., *Perceiving Women* (London: Dent and Sons, 1975), pp. 22–5.

22. W. E. B. Dubois, *The Souls of Black Folk* (New York: Random House, 1990), pp. 140–55.

23. See discussion in Estelle Lauter, *Women as Mythmakers* (Bloomington, IN: Indiana University Press, 1984), pp. 58–9.

24. C. G. Jung, *Collected Works,* vol. 10 (Princeton, NJ: Princeton University Press, 1970), paragraphs 93–94.

25. Benjamin, *Bonds of Love,* pp. 116–17.

26. John Gray, *Men Are from Mars, Women Are from Venus* (New York: Harper, 1993).

27. Sylvia Perera, *Descent to the Goddess* (Toronto: Inner City Books, 1981), p. 95.

28. C. G. Jung, "Aion," in *Collected Works,* vol. 9 (Princeton, NJ: Princeton University Press, 1968), pp. 11–22.

29. Andrew Samuels, "Gender and Psyche," *Anima* 11, no. 2: 136.

30. Andrew Samuels, *Jung and the Post-Jungians* (London: Routledge, 1985), pp. 212–15.

31. Samuels, *Jung,* p. 212.

32. Gilligan, *Crossroads,* p. 170.

33. C. G. Jung, *Collected Works,* vol. 17 (Princeton, NJ: Princeton University Press, 1968), pp. 189–201.

34. Adolf Guggenbühl-Craig, *Marriage: Dead or Alive* (Dallas: Spring Publications, 1977), pp. 22–34.

35. Samuels, *Jung,* p.102.

36. See Roberson Davies' novels for the most effective depiction of this concept, especially *What's Bred in the Bone* (New York: Viking, 1985).

37. Guggenbühl-Craig, *Marriage,* p. 22.

38. Ibid., p. 41.

39. Lauter, *Women,* p.76.

Chapter Four

1. Ovid, *Metamorphoses* (London: Penguin Books, 1988), p. 162.

2. Several versions of Medea's story give long lists of those she rejuvenated in the cauldron, ranging from an old ram to the nurses of the god Dionysus. (James Claus, *Medea* [Princeton, NJ: Princeton University Press, 1997], 34.) Rejuvenation is a change of status. To move from whole to dismembered to wholly new is to go through an initiation. An initiation incorporates three stages for the initiate: (1) detachment from a fixed social structure and identity; (2) entering a threshold state of ambiguity (liminality); (3) resolution into a new, very different identity. (Victor Turner, "The Liminal Period in the Rites of Passage," *Betwixt and Between,* eds. Mahdi, J. et al. [Lasalle, IL: Open Court, 1987], 7.) Presiding over this initiation, Medea may take you all the way through or abandon you part way, leaving you in the dismembered or liminal state. One can see this theme of dismemberment developing in Medea's story when she dismembers her half-brother before the cauldron appears, and it continues beyond the cauldron episodes to her vengeful acts in a coming episode of her story.

Dismemberment occurs in mythic narrative in two radically different forms. We can use the myths of Tiamat and Inanna to exemplify these two forms. Tiamat, "she who fashions all things," was a great Babylonian goddess. She was defeated in battle by Marduk, a god, hero, and avenger of "the fathers." "Whereafter he split her like a shellfish, in two halves: set one above as a heavenly roof. . . . He then established a great abode, the Earth." Joseph Campbell, *The Masks of God: Occidental Mythology* [New York: Arkana, 1991], 82–4.) Marduk goes on to order and rule all that Tiamat had made and all that was made from her mutilated body. Tiamat's dismemberment provides the prima materia for a new patriarchal world.

She is sacrificed and destroyed in the process, her very body converted to serve the ambitions of the patriarchal heroic ideal.

Inanna was the Sumerian "Queen of Heaven and Earth." Her dismemberment occurs in the course of an underworld journey which she voluntarily undertakes. Her initiation into the underworld requires her to be stripped. At each of the seven gates of the great below, Inanna is forced to give up another of her earthly attributes until she is a slab of meat rotting on a peg, a process reminiscent of crucifixion. Her dismemberment is an integral aspect of her encounter and reconciliation with the "dark sister" Ereshkigal, ruler of the underworld and a goddess of death and regeneration. Inanna undergoes a necessary deconstruction of her old configuration of self. She is reembodied and returns from the descent with a new stance toward her upperworld life, a stance that allows her to reconfigure her connection to the masculine powers of the upperworld, represented in the myth by her consort Dumuzi. Her dismemberment has occurred in the service of her own regeneration. This dismemberment in the underworld leads to rebirth.

According to Sylvia Perera, a Jungian analyst, Inanna's journey is the archetypal model of a process that is particularly important to women who have tried to form themselves in a patriarchal mold. She perceives the process as "an initiation essential for most modern women in the Western world; without it we are not whole. The process requires both a sacrifice of our identity as spiritual daughters of the patriarchy and a descent . . . because so much of the power and passion of the feminine has been dormant in the underworld—in exile for five thousand years." (Perera, *Descent,* p. 14.)

Although she sometimes uses dismemberment to consolidate power in the style of Marduk with Tiamat, for the most part we see Medea as an expert at initiations of rebirth, like that of Inanna. Medea as an initiatrix is "a persona who may have belonged to the prehistory of our extant myths." (Claus, p. 41.) That prehistory refers once again to shamanism, in this case to shamanistic images and rites of dismemberment. Experiences of skeletal dismemberment are an aspect of crossing over into the underworld that appear in the earliest known versions of hero journeys, those in which a tribal shaman enters an alternative reality in order to seek special healing or balancing knowledge. Again we find Medea's magic reaching back to the immanent worldview of the Great Goddess and farther back to the shamanic form of immanent conversation.

Medea's cauldron regenerates flesh and in that way it resembles the magical cauldron used by an Irish hero-King to continuously rejuvenate his slaughtered warriors and thus avoid defeat. Celtic myth expands this theme of rejuvenation from the body to the mind. When the cauldron is in the hands of a Celtic goddess like Cerridwen, it rejuvenates the mind and spirit, provides knowledge, insight, and inspiration. The muse of the Celtic bards was said to have emerged from the cauldron of Cerridwen. At one point Medea seems to refer to the cauldron's Celtic fame, pretending to Pelias that she has brought it from the "foggy land of the Hyperboreans," i. e., Britain. (Graves, v. 2, pp. 251–3.)

3. Carlo Ginzburg, *Ecstasies* (New York: Pantheon, 1991), pp. 300–7.

4. Jung, "Aion," p. 14.

5. Jung, *Collected Works*, vol. 10, paragraph 275.

6. As with many of Jung's theoretical concepts, his statements about Eros and Logos are contradictory. He states that Eros is woman's essential nature and Logos is man's. Then, in a later work, he acknowledges that the opposite can be true. (C. G. Jung, *Mysterium Conjunctionis* [Princeton, NJ: Princeton University Press, 1963], 179–80). However, in a famous instance of the "vision" seminars, he failed to put that insight into action. (See Claire Douglas's excellent analysis of this in her article, "Christiana Morgan's "Visions Reconsidered," *San Francisco Jung Institute Library Journal* 8, no. 4 [1989].)

In general practice, activities and traits that demonstrate Logos are highly valued and usually seen as masculine. Behavior and capacities which further Eros are depicted as very "other" and are classified as feminine. As Miller noted in our previous discussion, these aspects of the human experience are relegated increasingly to a realm outside of full awareness, where they are at worst denigrated, at best experienced as vague, undeveloped, and trivial. This skew in the comparative worth assigned to Eros and Logos has implications for individual, personal values, and implications on a broader scale, affecting our experience of meaning, the nature of our connection to the world, and our spiritual values.

7. Samuels, *Jung*, p. 219.

8. See John Peacock, *Pilgrims of Paradox: Calvinism and Experience among Primitive Baptists of the Blue Ridge* (Washington, DC: Smithsonian, 1989), and Lee Smith, *The Devil's Dream* (New York: Ballantine, 1993).

9. Elaine Pagels, *Adam, Eve, and the Serpent* (New York: Vintage, 1989), p. 147.

10. It was Jung's opinion that the hyperrational, materialist stance of the Western ego gives rise to a loss of meaning in the experience of life. (C. G. Jung, *Collected Works*, vol. 12 [Princeton, NJ: Princeton University Press, 1968], para 657.) The transcendent ideal alienates people from meanings that are felt rather than intellectually constructed; it invalidates meaningful experiences that are rooted and experienced in emotion, symbol, somatic experience, or spiritual life. Emphasis on personal autonomy, control, and individualism as the psychological norms causes the individual to be isolated, alienated from others and from the natural world. Nature, whether experienced in the earth or in the body, cannot be controlled by individual willpower. The individual human being is vulnerable to nature; we are small in its scheme. Transcendent ideals will not acknowledge this fact, promoting instead a grandiose image of the human being in relationship to nature. This is one of the reasons that "people socialized in the modern world view emerge as strangers in the cosmos." (Charlene Spretnak, "Embodied, Embedded Philosophy," *Open Eye* 12, no. 1 [1995]: 4–6.) And often these strangers begin looking for a home in what is perceived as the realm of the Feminine.

11. Pagels, *Adam*, pp. 147–8.

12. Todd Berger, "Lost in Space," *San Francisco Examiner Magazine*, May 4, 1997, pp. 34–8.

13. Beginning in classical Greece, where the foundation of Western culture was laid, we find, according to Naomi Goldenberg, that "the best things about the world are somehow not of the world." (Naomi Goldenberg, *Returning Words to Flesh* [Boston: Beacon Press, 1991], 206.) The ego ideal of Western culture is mirrored in (or may have its roots in) a particular relationship to nature. The ideal man in the West, according to Richard Tarnas, "has been a questing masculine hero who has constantly striven to differentiate himself from and control the matrix out of which he emerged . . . [He is] driven by an heroic impulse to forge an autonomous rational human self by separating it from the primordial unity with nature." (Richard Tarnas, *The Passion of the Western Mind* [New York: Harmony Books, 1991], 441.) The hero uses Logos to transcend nature, whose operating principle is Eros. Nature, as an immanent spiritual presence is, from the heroic perspective, a primitive threat or a trivial impediment. True meaning in life lies in transcendence of nature. That transcendence can be reached through the religious pursuit of

purity, the philosophical pursuit of absolute truth, the scientific pursuit of objective knowledge, or, in late twentieth-century America, perhaps transcendence is sought through the gymnastic pursuit of a perfect body. In this dualistic perspective, the divine or sacred elements of life, those which hold the highest meaning, are completely separate from the material elements of life.

Culture's prevailing definition of the divine—its nature and quality—strongly affects the individual's sense of what is meaningful in life. The psychological experience of meaning is bound up with the cultural assignment of sacrality. I think that this is true even for people who hold no particular religious beliefs, who have a secular worldview. The secular worldview is a fairly recent phenomenon, and the Western world's value system has very old, primarily religious, roots. Religious scholar Elaine Pagels attributes the prevalence of certain values in modern Western culture to the dominance of St. Augustine's dogma. This dogma was originally adopted by the Roman Empire as orthodoxy in the fifth century. Pagels believes that the long-term hegemony of the Augustine worldview, enforced by the state and the Inquisition, has caused it to become embedded as an assumption dominating the collective Western worldview, regardless of the specific, conscious religious beliefs or nonbeliefs of contemporary individuals or countries. (Elaine Pagels, *Adam, Eve, and the Serpent* [New York: Vintage, 1989], 147.) Augustine's system of values was relentlessly transcendent. Life breaks down hierarchically into two categories, the transcendent and the immanent. In the less worthy category, the immanent, we find the female associated with the corporeal, earthly, irrational, and constricted. In the nobler category, the transcendent, we find the male associated with the spiritual, heavenly, rational, and expansive. (Gillian Clarke, *Women in Late Antiquity* [Oxford: Oxford University Press, 1993], 124.) Although the incorporation of this worldview into state-supported church dogma may have "nailed it down" in Western culture, it is a view that predates Christianity.

What are immanent values? What is immanence? It is the divine within the material, the sacred in the everyday. According to Charlene Spretnak, a writer who is deeply involved in the revival of goddess spirituality, the immanent worldview portrays "culture as not in opposition to nature but as a potentially harmonious extension of nature . . . reflective of . . the teachings of nature: diversity, subjectivity, adaptability, interrelatedness . . . Instead of accepting the idea that one must transcend the body and nature, it is possible to apprehend divine transcendence as the sacred whole, or the infinite complexity of the universe." She associates this view with the image of the ancient Great Goddess who "expresses ongoing regeneration within the cycles of her Earthbody." (Spretnek, "Ecofeminism," p. 12–15.) The movement to renew goddess spirituality portrays immanence as a female form of the sacred.

Immanent spirituality is also manifest in other groups that operate outside the dominant value system. Certain groups—I am thinking primarily of indigenous people who have maintained a traditional, tribal culture—have retained or recovered cultural practices, rituals and beliefs that reflect an immanent worldview. In that worldview, "there is here no knower and known, no subject and object. Rather there are actors in relationships of mutuality. By acting one transforms not only the world but oneself. Therefore, it is a fundamentally dynamic world, always moving always changing always in flux." (Frederique Apffel-Marglin, "Development or Decolonization in the Andes," *Daybreak* 4, no. 3 [1994]: 9.) Anthropologists have defined this relationship to the world as "participation mystique," the phenomenon of experiencing a personal identification, a "oneness" with nature, with other people, with the spiritual, with what Jung called the *anima mundi* or "world soul." In participation mystique, subject and object are united. The concept of participation mystique is a useful shorthand and one that Jung uses frequently. However, it is somewhat tainted by the implication, in both anthropological and psychological literature, that those who experience participation mystique, have, in some way, a more primitive consciousness than those who read about the experience. For this reason, I prefer Kremer's term, "immanent conversation," a process in which "individuals understand themselves to be in an ongoing conversation with the surrounding community, in which the local animals, plants, . . . and spirits . . . take as much part as other humans." (Jürgen Kremer, "The Shadow of Evolutionary Thinking," *Revision* 19, no. 1 [Summer 1996]: 47.) Here we see the malleable boundaries and interdependency associated with the psychology of women expanded to a relationship with the world itself.

To be in immanent conversation with the world is profoundly "other" to the Western ego ideal of rationality, autonomy, objectivity, and control. In fact, as Richard Tarnas states in *The Passion of the Western Mind,* "The evolution of the Western mind has been founded on the repression of the feminine, [the repression] of the Participation Mystique with nature: a progressive denial of the anima mundi, of the soul of the world, of the community of being, of mystery and ambiguity, of imagination, emotion, instinct, body, nature, woman." (Tarnes, *Western Mind,* p. 441.)

14. See discussion of this in Elinor Gadon, *The Once and Future Goddess* (San Francisco: Harper & Row, 1989), pp. 190–4.

15. Sylvia Perera, *The Scapegoat Complex* (Toronto: Inner City Books, 1986), pp. 50–2.

16. Vilification of the female body in Western theology has contributed to its cultural use as a symbolic container for that which is irrational, tainted, dangerous, chaotic, engulfing, and out of control. When an individual female body fits the culture's visual ideal, it may hold these qualities as an alluring, freeing alternative to the alienating prison of hyperrationality and constant control that characterizes culture's dominant, masculinized way of being. When the individual female body varies from the current fashionable ideal as all real life bodies do, it holds these qualities as a repulsive embodiment of the threatening "other." This meaning-image of the body is deeply introjected by most women in Western cultures.

In my own psychotherapy practice, I have noted that, for women, self-hatred lives most fundamentally and intractably in the body. This basic reality contributes in an obvious way to the eating disorders and exercise disorders which are endemic among women. It contributes less obviously, but perhaps seminally, to a wide range of debilitating distortions of identity and self-image that women suffer, a range which might be summed up as forms of self-loathing. Many forms of self-loathing originate in bodily experiences such as child abuse and incest. Even when the roots of distorted self-image lie elsewhere, the body may easily become the repository of the feeling experience of self-hatred. As a consequence most women feel that the body must be molded, disciplined, and scrutinized but also, paradoxically, ignored as a source of joy or wisdom.

17. See Naomi Wolf, *The Beauty Myth* (New York: Doubleday, 1996).

18. Jessica Benjamin, *Like Subjects and Love Objects: Essays on Recognition and Sexual Difference* (New Haven, CT: Yale University Press, 1995), p. 138.

19. Robert Graves, *The Greek Myths*, vol. 2 (New York: Viking Penguin, 1975), p. 333.

20. Ibid., pp. 56–7.

21. Clauss, *Medea*, p. 72.

22. Graves, *Greek Myths*, vol. 1, pp. 56–7.

23. For Circe's complete story, see Graves, *Greek Myths*, vol. 2, pp. 358–60.

24. Clauss, *Medea,* p. 87.

25. Four millennia ago, patriarchal nomadic conquests in Greece and the Levant overcame ancient matriarchal cultures. These prepatriarchal cultures had been centered around the worship of Great Goddesses who embodied the divine within nature, within the material world. Such goddess figures were notable for the way in which they combined qualities that Western culture now sees as contradictory. We have already looked at a number of elements in Medea's story that indicate her association with these ancient goddess figures. The cauldron itself is a symbol of the power of the goddess, portraying a potent mix of destruction, regeneration, flux, and movement in and out of strict categories.

26. Estelle Lauter sees the reemergence in Western culture of the archetypal image of the goddess as marking "recurrent questions about female experience. . . . These images mark generative experiences of problems that occur without being completely solved." (Estelle Lauter, *Women as Mythmakers,* pp. 208–9.) Her view connects back to Miller's notion of the connection between women and the dominant culture's unsolved problems, but she views that connection as "generative," not just burdensome. Lauter thinks that a spontaneous surge of mythic imagery, as with contemporary images of the goddess, marks the gap between inner possibility and outer reality, the intersection between what is manifest and what is potential.

27. Guggenbühl-Craig, *Marriage,* pp. 22–34.

28. Miller, *Psychology of Women,* p. 112.

29. Peter Gomes is quoted by Robert Boynton in "God and Harvard," *New Yorker,* 11 November 1996, pp. 64–70.

Chapter Five

1. Patricia Bosworth, "Goodbye, Connecticut," *New York Times Book Review,* 13 October 1996, p. 7.

2. Daphne Merkin, "The Years with Roth," *New Yorker,* 4 November 1996, p. 102.

3. Friedan, *Feminine Mystique.*

4. Gary Wills, "All the Pope's Men," *New Yorker,* 2 December 1996, p. 110.

5. Jung, "Aion," pp. 11–12.

6. See the introduction to every article in Jordan et al. (eds.), *Women's Growth in Connection.*

7. "The law of Eros requires that one's own desires shall not be taken as absolutes but shall be adapted to the needs and desires of the other person and to the requirements of the situation." (Esther Harding, *Women's Mysteries* [New York: Harper & Row, 1971], 143.) If women are identified with the purposes of Eros in some of the ways we have discussed, they may surrender themselves because of the archetypal drive of Eros to produce relatedness. Despite the fact that Eros manifests primarily through relationships, there is a curiously impersonal quality to Eros, especially in the way it is collectively imagined as a function of the feminine. Eros requires that we be in the midst of other peoples lives, connected to them in the most visceral possible ways, but it does not require that we know who they really are. Mere relatedness is not genuine relationship. One can be deeply involved with another person without seeing that person with any accuracy.

8. Gilligan, *Crossroads,* p. 203.

9. Ibid., p. 215.

10. Ibid., p. 216.

11. See Claire Bloom, *Leaving a Doll's House* (Boston: Little, Brown & Company, 1996).

12. Miller, *Toward a New Psychology,* p. 23. According to Jung, "The psychic totality, the self, is a combination of opposites. Without a shadow even the self is not real." (C. G. Jung, *Collected Works,* vol. 10 [Princeton, NJ: Princeton University Press, 1970], 337.) The relationship between the ego, which for most people is the acknowledged "I," and the unconscious is typically dominated by what Jung calls the "shadow problem." The shadow—the personal experiences, feelings, and attributes that are most inimical to the ego ideal—sits at the entrance to the unconscious, like the paralyzing river Styx at the entrance to the underworld. In order to gain access to the inner guidance and resources of the self the ego must come to a modus vivendi with the shadow. Traditional Jungian theory holds that images of the shadow are always of the same gender as the ego. I think that the stories we have been working with show us something different for issues of masculine gender role and with masculine imagery.

13. Perera, *Scapegoat,* p. 51. The personal shadow is, of course, affected by the cultural shadow, but issues of the personal shadow must be worked through by each individual. No cultural or societal change will relieve an individual of his or her shadow problem. In an adult, the relationships

between parts of the self, such as the ego and the shadow, are internalized, embedded. Conscious effort must be made to shift those relationships. The ego's stance toward the self is unconsciously modeled on the parents' stance toward the child's emerging individuality. The ego's stance toward the shadow, which guides the intrapsychic relationship between ego and shadow, is more specifically based on the parents' attitude toward those aspects of the child that the parents found troublesome, unlikable, inconvenient, or that they simply did not notice or know how to respond to. These parts of the self had to be dismissed and disdained to in order to fulfill a role in the family's system. The individual's internalized stance toward the shadow, modeled on familial attitudes, must shift. When it does, the ego and the shadow come into a new relationship, a relationship that gives the ego greater access to the Self.

14. For an excellent discussion of the association of danger with males, see Robert Sapolsky, *The Trouble with Testosterone* (New York: Simon & Schuster, 1997).

15. Lang, *Fairy Book,* pp. 292–4.

16. Some victims of abuse and oppression communicate the repressed shadow dimensions of that experience through a passive-into-active process. She assumes the active role in interpersonal drama when formerly she had been forced into the passive role. She unconsciously puts others in the position she was in—the one whose self does not count. She does this through direct and indirect pressure, both verbal and nonverbal.

Chapter Six

1. Clauss, *Medea,* p. 82.

2. Phillip Harriman (ed.), *Dictionary of Psychology,* s.v. "repetition compulsion" (New York: Philosophical Library, 1947), p. 289.

3. Perera, *Scapegoat,* p. 51.

4. Tannen, *Don't Understand,* p. 255.

5. Joseph Campbell, *The Masks of God: Primitive Mythology* (New York: Penguin, 1985), p. 273.

6. *The Complete Grimms' Fairy Tales* (New York: Pantheon, 1972), pp. 216–19.

7. C. G. Jung, *Freud and Psychoanalysis,* vol. 4 of *Collected Works* (Princeton, NJ: Princeton University Press, 1985), p. 255.

8. Children become internal shapeshifters. All children employ altered states both to play and to defend themselves against the internal effects of experiences that might otherwise be intolerable. States of dissociation are available to all children. These include living in a fantasy world; derealization (a state in which events do not feel real); depersonalization (a state in which the child does not experience himself or herself as real); and time relativity (a state in which time speeds up or alternatively stands still). Most adults remember such states of consciousness as part of the magic of childhood and the freedom of play. This may account for many of the "lost paradise" images we have of childhood in general.

9. Jung, *Freud and Psychoanalysis,* pp. 255–6.

10. Ellen Fein and Sherrie Schneider, *The Rules* (New York: Warner Books, 1996).

11. Ron Messer, "A Jungian Interpretation of the Relationship of Culture, Hero, and Trickster," *Studies in Religion* 2, no. 3 (1982): 310.

12. R. Bosnak, *A Little Course in Dreams* (Boston: Shambhala, 1993), p. 64.

13. Robert Hopcke, *A Guided Tour to the Collected Works of Jung* (Boston: Shambhala, 1992), pp. 95–8.

14. Jung, *Psychological Reflections,* p. 256.

Chapter Seven

1. Ethel Phelps, *The Maid of the North* (New York: Henry Holt, 1981), pp. 97–106.

2. Gilligan, *Crossroads,* p. 112.

3. Alice Miller, *The Drama of the Gifted Child: How Narcissistic Parents Form and Deform the Emotional Lives of their Talented Children* (New York: Basic Books, 1981), p. 68.

4. Gilligan, *Crossroads,* p. 226.

5. Charlotte Brontë, *Jane Eyre* (New York: Dutton, 1960).

6. Gilligan, *Crossroads,* p. 203.

7. Abigail Van Buren, "Dear Abby," *San Francisco Chronicle,* 30 July 1997, sec. A, p. 12.

8. Gilligan, *Crossroads,* p. 112.

9. Ibid., p. 215.

10. Freud's work is, of course, the most infamous in this regard, particularly in *Some Psychical Consequences of the Anatomical Distinction between the Sexes,* vol. 19 in *Collected Works* (London: Hogarth Press, 1961), pp. 257–8. Lawrence Kohlberg has also contributed to this view in his work, "Continuities and Discontinuities in Child and Adult Moral Development," *Human Development* 12 (1960): 93–120.

11. Samuels, Jung, pp. 231–2.

12. C. G. Jung, *Collected Works,* vol. 11 (Princeton, NJ: Princeton University Press, 1968), pp. 411–13.

13. Hopcke, *Guided Tour,* p. 126

14. See Carolyn Heilbrun, *The Last Gift of Time* (New York: Dial, 1997). See also Patricia Holt, "Books," *San Francisco Chronicle,* 29 April 1997, sec. B, p. 4.

15. Ann Ulanov, *The Feminine* (Evanston, IL: Northwestern University Press, 1971), p. 340.

INDEX

About the Author

Tanya Wilkinson is Professor of Psychology and Core Faculty Member at the California Institute of Integral Studies in San Francisco and a licensed psychotherapist in private practice. Specializing in women's issues and Jungian psychology, Dr. Wilkinson provides clinical training and conducts workshops, and has received the Distinguished Teaching Award at CIIS. *Medea's Folly* is her second book. Her previous title is *Persephone Returns: Victims, Heroes, and the Journey from the Underworld.* In addition to teaching, writing, and counseling, she is a fine artist specializing in mixed media. Dr. Wilkinson received her Ph.D. in Psychology from the California School of Professional Psychology. She resides in San Francisco, California.

PAGEMILL PRESS publishes books primarily in the field of psychology, with an eye to personal growth. Our authors explore the intellectual, psychological, and spiritual dimensions of our daily lives—the connection between mind and body, the power of myth and dreams in everyday circumstances, the role of the unconscious in human interactions, the wisdom and insight the body has to offer our total health, and the integration of a fuller experience of the body in life's activities.

For a catalog of our publications or editorial submissions, please write:

PAGEMILL PRESS
2716 Ninth Street
Berkeley, CA 94710
Phone: (510) 848-3600
Fax: (510) 848-1326
E-mail: Circulus@aol.com